Spreading the Fire

Sr. Mary Joanne Wittenburg, SND

ISBN: 1475257120
ISBN-13: 9781475257120

Introduction

The Eleven Pioneers

In the late 1990s, the world was approaching the Third Millennium and the Sisters of Notre Dame, the 150th anniversary of their Congregation. Sister Mary Sujita Kallupurakkathu, S.N.D. their Superior General, drew attention to the words of Jesus: "I have come to cast fire on the earth and how I long to see it burn brightly." (Luke 12:49)

What is this Fire of which Jesus speaks? It is the Fire for Mission. It is the Fire that was ignited in the hearts of twenty-two year old Hilligonde Wolbring and her friend, twenty-eight year old Elisabeth Kuhling when, in 1850, they received the habit and Rule of the Sisters of Notre Dame. It is the Fire which a small group of Religious Women carried to the United States in 1874, choosing exile from their homeland, Germany, rather than accept the anti-religious laws of Bismarck's *Kulturkampf* and the dissolution of their Congregation.

It is the fire which eleven Sisters of Notre Dame brought to Southern California in 1924.

Spreading the Fire is an account of the challenges and accomplishments of the Sisters of Notre Dame during their eighty-six years of ministry in California. However, this narrative is not simply a history. It is the story of the Fire – this passion for the mission of Jesus – as reflected in the lives of these Religious Women as they forged the spirit that characterizes the Province of Rosa Mystica today. Moreover, it is a tribute to the sisters, past and present, who inherited the Fire, nurtured it and continue to spread its flames.

Chapter One

Beginnings

At the beginning of the twentieth century, Los Angeles was a relatively small town. The National Census of 1910 registered a population of slightly less than 320,000 individuals.[1] In 1913, however, William Mulholland completed construction of the Owens River Aqueduct, thereby multiplying Los Angeles' water supply five-fold. As a result, between 1910 and 1930, the city increased the size of its territory ten times. The amount of irrigated farm land rose from 3,000 acres in 1914 to 75,000 in 1917. Suddenly Los Angeles began to move toward the status of a metropolis.

Freed from the restraints of World War I, waves of immigrants, chiefly from the mid-west, poured into the region. Although the promise of cheap land as well as the employment opportunities offered by the burgeoning motion picture industry, and by oil strikes in Long Beach, Huntington Beach and Santa Fe Springs contributed to the influx, many people were lured west by Los Angeles' warm Mediterranean climate.

Among those impressed by Southern California's mild weather was Reverend Mother Mary Cecilia Romen, third Superior General of the Sisters of Notre Dame (1895-1925), who wanted to establish a house "in the country" where sisters who suffered from the harsh winters in Ohio and Kentucky could regain their health. The possibility of opening such a house in California

---

1   Fifteenth Census of the United States, 1930 Populations: Number and Distribution of Inhabitants, Volume One, 22. Department of   Social Sciences – Philosophy – Religion, Richard J. Riordan Central Library, Los Angeles.

had not entered Reverend Mother Mary Cecilia's mind until Sister Mary Anthony Honeck, District Superior in Covington, Kentucky, forwarded a letter to her in 1923 from Mrs. Catherine Pohl of Huntington Park. It contained an intriguing invitation: "Our pastor, Father Patrick Pearse [sic][2] is asking for Sisters for the school in our parish, St. Matthias. Would your Sisters consider this tempting offer, and come to California?"[3]

Mrs. Pohl's letter was quickly followed by one from The Right Reverend John J. Cantwell[4] giving the sisters permission to enter his diocese and extending a personal invitation to Reverend Mother Mary Cecilia to visit Los Angeles.[5] Bishop Cantwell's letter of welcome prompted the following response which set the tone for the Congregation's future relationship with the California hierarchy:

> Our Sisters will earnestly endeavor to assist Father Pierse in his labors for the salvation of souls, and the educa-

2   Father Patrick Pierse (1887-1964) was born in Ireland on February 7, 1887 and ordained a priest there on May 26, 1912. He ministered in St. Monica Parish, Santa Monica (1912-1917), and in St. Paul Parish in Colinga, Fresno County (1917-1919) before being named pastor of St. Matthias Parish in 1919. In 1926, Father Pierse was appointed pastor of St. Clement Parish, Santa Monica (1926-1951). He next served as pastor of St. Boniface Parish, Anaheim (1951-1958) and finally of St. Peter Parish, Los Angeles (1958-1964). Father Pierse died in March 1964 at the age of 77 years.
3   Quoted in Sister Mary Vincentia Klein, S.N.D., Their Quiet Tread, Milwaukee: Bruce Press, 1955, 320. Mrs. Pohl did not know the Sisters of Notre Dame personally. However, she was a friend of a Mrs. Charles Nissen, a former pupil of the sisters in Carrolltown, Kentucky, who told her about the community…Shortly afterward, Reverend Mother Mary Cecilia received a formal invitation from Father Pierse himself. Father Pierse also sent $200 to defray the travel expenses for herself and a companion so that she could evaluate the situation in Huntington Park in person.
4   The Right Reverend John J. Cantwell was installed as fifth bishop of the Diocese of Monterey-Los Angeles on December 12, 1917. In June 1922 the area north and east of Santa Barbara County was organized into the Diocese of Monterey-Fresno. The remaining 44,353 square miles became the Diocese of Los Angeles-San Diego. Twelve years later, in December 1936, the southern four counties were incorporated into the newly erected Diocese of San Diego. At the same time, the Holy See raised the remaining counties of Santa Barbara, Ventura, Los Angeles and Orange — approximately 9,544 square miles — to the status of an archdiocese with Bishop Cantwell as archbishop. The Right Reverend John J. Cantwell died on October 30, 1947.
5   This letter is not among Archbishop Cantwell's papers in the Archival Center of the Archdiocese of Los Angeles. Its contents are implied from Reverend Mother Mary Cecilia's response.

tion of youth, conformable in all things to his wishes and direction. I am confident that he will be a true Father to the few sisters so far away from their higher Superiors, while the kind interest of your Lordship in supporting and furthering their labors, will be an incentive to them, and a great consolation to me. I am convinced that in every difficulty and need, the Sisters can count on your fatherly counsel and solicitude.[6]

In the same letter, Reverend Mother Mary Cecilia offered another reason for her interest in extending the community's ministry to Southern California:

I trust that the bright outlook for vocations expressed in your letter, Right Reverend and dear Bishop, will be realized, for it was just this expectation that decided our acceptance of this new and promising field of labor. For the accomplishment of this end, we shall fervently pray.[7]

Reverend Mother Mary Cecilia also promised "to make a personal inspection of [the] new mission…in the winter" adding "if God gives me health and strength, as this will be a necessary condition for so long a journey at the age of seventy-one."[8]

Poor health as well as the affairs of the new foundation in Brazil kept Reverend Mother Mary Cecilia in Ohio and Kentucky for the next several months. As a result, it was not until December 1923 that she was able to take the first steps toward establishing a house on the west coast.

At that time, Mrs. Arthur O'Neill and her son, Felix, both of whom lived in Long Beach, a city south of Los Angeles, were

---

6   5 [Reverend] Mother M. Cecilia, Letter to The Right Reverend John J. Cantwell, August 3, 1923. Archival Center, Archdiocese of Los Angeles. Cited hereinafter as AALA. Although the letter, was written by Reverend Mother Mary Cecilia, it was signed by Sister Mary Antonie [Sommer] who added a postscript, dated September 24, 1923, in which she explained that the delay in responding to Bishop Cantwell's letter was due to the "sudden serious illness of our Mother General."

7   Ibid.

8   Ibid.

visiting her daughter, Sister Mary Josita, in Toledo, Ohio.[9]   At the same time, Sister Mary Bernard Flury, superior of St. Paul Convent in Norwalk, Ohio, was in Cleveland undergoing medical tests.   Reverend Mother Mary Cecilia asked the O'Neills if Sister Mary Bernard and Sister Mary Josita could return to California with them.   Not only would Sister Mary Bernard benefit from the milder climate but, at the same time, she could look over the situation in Huntington Park and open negotiations with Father Pierse for the community's acceptance of his parish school if feasible.

Arrangements were quickly made. And on January 7, 1924, the two sisters, together with the O'Neills, boarded the train in Toledo enroute to Los Angeles. The temperature that day registered sixteen degrees below zero. Sister Mary Bernard later recorded her delight as the snow-covered cities, plains and mountains gradually gave way to palm trees, orange groves and flowers.[10]

Upon their arrival in Long Beach, Mr. O'Neill rented a small house on Lime Avenue for the two sisters and placed his car and driver at their disposal. The house itself was located only a few blocks from St. Anthony Church where a Capuchin priest from St. Lawrence of Brindisi Parish in South Los Angeles, Father Joseph Fenelon, O.F.M., Cap. was giving a men's retreat. After meeting the sisters and learning the reason for their trip to Southern California, Father decided to contact Reverend Mother Mary Cecilia in Cleveland himself and ask for sisters for his own parochial school.

In the meantime, Reverend Mother Mary Cecilia was completing her own arrangements to visit California. Sister Mary Bernard and Sister Mary Josita had hoped to find rooms for their guests at St. Mary's Hospital in Long Beach but none were available.   Since the cottage on Lime Avenue was too small to ac-

---

9   Sister Mary Josita [Catherine O'Neill] was the youngest of Arthur and Marie O'Neill's three daughters, all of whom entered the Sisters of Notre Dame. Their oldest girl, Margaret Mary [Sister Mary Clare] had been assigned to St. Paul School in Norwalk in 1917 as principal and teacher. Therefore, Sister Mary Bernard, who was superior there (1911-1924) was well known to the O'Neill family.

10   Cited in Sister Mary Louise Wanamaker, S.N.D., <u>Biography of Sister Mary Bernard: 1882-1966</u>, Rosa Mystica Province, Thousand Oaks, California, August 1994, 20-21. Archives of the Sisters of Notre Dame, Thousand Oaks, California. Cited hereinafter as ASNDTO.

commodate three additional people, the sisters rented a small apartment on the corner of 7th and Lime Avenues for Reverend Mother and her companions, just three blocks north of where they themselves were living.

Unfortunately, the dampness of the weather acerbated Reverend Mother Mary Cecilia's rheumatism. Furthermore, the distance from Long Beach to Los Angeles proved to be inconvenient for business meetings in the city. Consequently, shortly before Sister Mary Bernard and Sister Mary Josita left Southern California, Reverend Mother Mary Cecilia, Sister Mary Antonie and Sister Mary Methodia moved to a small bungalow on Sunset Boulevard near Blessed Sacrament Church in Hollywood which was much closer to downtown Los Angeles.

On Tuesday, March 11, 1924, Mother Mary Cecilia and two companions, Sister Mary Antonie Sommer and Sister Mary Methodia Dorenkamp arrived in Los Angeles.[11] Once there, Reverend Mother Mary Cecilia wasted no time finalizing plans for the new foundation. After resting a few days, she paid a visit to Father Pierse at St. Matthias Parish. On March 15, 1924, Reverend Mother Mary Cecilia, together with Sister Mary Antonie and Sister Mary Bernard, called upon Bishop Cantwell.

During the ensuing days, Reverend Mother Mary Cecilia found time to visit the various places in the diocese which Bishop Cantwell had mentioned as possible sites for future ministry: Holy Family Parish in Glendale, St. Dominic Parish in Eagle Rock, St. Augustine Parish in Culver City and St. Rita Parish in Sierra Madre.[12] However, in a letter dated May 1924, she warned the sisters in Cleveland:

---

11   Sister Mary Antonie Sommer was Reverend Mother Mary Cecilia's secretary; Sister Mary Methodia Dorenkamp, her nurse.
A detailed description of their trip will be found in a letter from Mother Mary Cecilia to the sisters in Cleveland, dated May 1924. Archives of the Sisters of Notre Dame, Chardon, Ohio. Cited hereinafter as ASNDC
12   Reverend Mother Mary Cecilia also visited Altadena, Van Nuys, Burbank and Tujunga.
Sister M. Antonie, S.N.D., Letter to Sister Superior [Mary Evarista Harks], February 21, 1925. ASNDC. Cited hereinafter as Letter, February 21, 1925. ASNDC

You must not think that it is my intention to open all these schools…we are going about this undertaking very slowly. I only looked upon it as my duty, since God called me here apparently for His own designs, without any effort on my part, -- that I get acquainted with the conditions of the country and the people living here in the West. If then, perhaps in the course of time, our work in this part of the U.S. expands, I would be in a better position to understand the needs and conditions peculiar to this part of the country.[13]

Since Reverend Mother Mary Cecilia was in California, Sister Mary Bernard and Sister Mary Josita made their own plans to return to Ohio. However, as Sister Mary Bernard later wrote, they were sorry to give up the "intimate talks and visits with dear Reverend Mother and companions, but …anxious to get back to normal living."[14]

By the time Reverend Mother Mary Cecilia herself left Southern California in May the number of proposed foundations had increased to two. Toward the end of April, Father Joseph Fenelon, O.F.M. had paid his promised visit to Reverend Mother Mary Cecilia and invited her to inspect the school and convent at St. Lawrence of Brindisi Parish. Reverend Mother Mary Cecilia gladly agreed to Father's request for sisters, since she believed two foundations, so far from the rest of the community in Ohio, could mutually support one another.[15]

During the summer months preparations for the new houses in California progressed steadily but for the most part secretly. Rumors concerning possible foundations on the west coast cir-

---

13   Mother Mary Cecilia, Letter to My dear Sisters, May 1924. Cited hereinafter as Letter, May 1924. ASNDC.

14   Cited in Sister Mary Joanne Wittenburg, S.N.D. [formerly Sister Mary Ste. Therese], House of Love, Rosa Mystica Province, Thousand Oaks, California, 1975, 3. ASNDTO. Cited hereinafter as Wittenburg, House, ASNDTO.

15   A more detailed description of Reverend Mother Mary Cecilia's stay in Southern California will be found in the letter: [Sister] M. Antonie, S.N.D., Letter to Sister M. Bonaventura et al., March 26, 1924. Translated from the German by Sister Mary Angelisita Lechner. S.N.D. ASNDTO.

culated among the sisters, but no definite details as to when and where were forthcoming until Reverend Mother Mary Cecilia read the appointments for 1924-1925 to the sisters at the provincial house on Ansel Road. She began by announcing: Then she read the names of the eleven pioneers. Sister Mary Bernard Flury, Sister Mary Hildegarde Delahanty, Sister Mary Isabel Lang, Sister Mary Walburge Schmitt, Sister Mary Ellen Healy and Sister Mary Amandis Kovac would be stationed at St. Matthias Parish in Huntington Park. Sister Mary Balbina Hagedorn, Sister Mary Clarissa Westhoven, Sister Mary Alice Lang, Sister Mary Sirana Kirchner and Sister Mary Blanche Wolf were assigned to St. Lawrence of Brindisi Parish in Watts.

"The Eleven"

Mother Mary Evarista Harks

Who were these women who laid the foundation for the ministry of the Sisters of Notre Dame in California? At first glance nothing extraordinary seems to mark their lives. Nevertheless, three qualities stand out – their spirit of prayer, their fidelity to religious life, and their love of community. Of Sister Mary Hildegarde Delahanty, it was written: "Sister's religious life was characterized by an…unusual spirit of prayer."[16] In her last years in the infirmary "she never seemed to tire of praying." Sister Mary Sirana Kirchner was described as "a powerful woman of prayer;" a "real community woman, as exemplified by her happy and yet deeply spiritual attitude;" a woman "generous, silent, whole-hearted and loyal," "highly respected by priests and lay persons, but most unassuming, humble and charitable in word and act." Sister Mary Walburge Schmitt was remembered for her "fidelity in her prayer life, devotion to duty, and concern for the community;" "in her humble, simple way, she went about her life of love through fidelity to little things, a love that required of her the most punctual and exact fulfillment of every single duty." Sister Mary Isabel Lang was known as a woman who lived "a simple, unassuming life – faithful to the exercise of her religious duties and of charity;" Sister Mary Amandis Kovac, as a person known for "her quiet, unassuming manner, and her gentle, kindly attention," who always performed her work "so quietly, so benignly and so well." Sister Mary Clarissa Westhoven was remembered as a "tiny person…characterized by a childlike simplicity and kindliness," someone "who placed a great value on opportunities for small, hidden acts of virtue," and as a "woman greatly devoted to community life."

This last quality, devotion to community life, was especially apparent in Sister Mary Blanche Wolf. Her sisters saw her as someone "known to be happy and cheerful, ready to sacrifice self for the sake of others, and possessed of an unusual sense of humor which made her the life of many a recreation and one of the chief entertainers on community feast days."

In addition to these gifts, each sister brought with her to California an openness of spirit, an abiding trust in God's goodness and provident care and a preferential love for the poor. For both Sister Mary Walburge and Sister Mary Clarissa pioneering in California was similar to being sent to the foreign missions. In later years, Sister Mary Walburge admitted that her appointment had not caused her any undue concern. She

---

16   This quotation and subsequent ones are taken from the obituaries of the respective sisters. ASNDC and ASNDTO.

had previously volunteered to go to China or India; Southern California would not be that much different.

This attitude is not difficult to understand. Rome had only removed the United States' status as a mission country in 1908. In fact, many women including Sister Mary Alvin Kastner, Sister Mary Antonita Biegansky, Sister Mary Manetia Weber and Sister Mary Floriberta Bast had entered the Congregation in Germany hoping to be sent to "the foreign missions," that is, to the United States. Being sent to California was seen as an expression of that call.

For Sister Mary Clarissa, her ministry in St. Lawrence of Brindisi Parish offered a unique opportunity to demonstrate her preferential love for the poor.

> She took to her kind heart the little children of the first and second grades whose cultural and social background was so radically different. She tried to understand them and help them. Through the children she endeavored to reach the parents and bring them closer to God and the church....In the 15 years Sister Mary Clarissa spent at St. Lawrence, her zeal never diminished.[17]

Originally, "The Eleven," as they called themselves, planned to leave for Los Angeles on August 19th but, because it was difficult to make train reservations for so many individuals, their departure was delayed a week.[18] In the interim, Sister Mary Bernard, with the help of Sister Mary Balbina and many sisters at the provincial house, collected and packed last minute items for the two new foundations.

Departure Day, August 26, 1924, finally arrived. The sisters, accompanied by Sister Mary Odila Miller and Sister Mary Adeline Gilhooly, arrived at the Erie Street Station in Cleveland only to

---

17   Obituary of Sister Mary Clarissa Westhoven, S.N.D. ASNDC.

18   Nearly all the traveling in the early days was done by means of free passes or half-fares solicited from the railroads. Bishop Cantwell himself had obtained such a pass for Reverend Mother Mary Cecilia when she and her companions returned to Ohio in the spring. He also obtained passes for four of the eleven sisters traveling to Los Angeles the following August.

discover that in the excitement of saying good-bye the suitcase containing their lunches for the five-day journey had been left behind. The loss created a good deal of consternation. Sister Mary Bernard shared her thoughts about their predicament in a letter to Mother Mary Evarista[19] and the sisters at the provincial house, dated August 29, 1924.

> All those precious lunches – they cost so much – now we have to buy food anyway and it's so expensive in the train and we need the money so badly. I'm sure those new lots on Green Road [the site of Notre Dame College] aren't paid for yet – then just think what the buildings are going to cost – and now our lunches are gone too. Will it all be wasted? There is really no way of getting [them] either. It would be a miracle for no [car] could beat the train.[20]

There was nothing for the sisters to do but board the train and resign themselves to the loss. But no sooner had they pulled into the 55th Street Station than Sister Mary Bernard's miracle occurred. The train had barely stopped when the sisters caught sight of Sister Mary Odila and Sister Mary Adeline hurrying toward their car, carrying the suitcase with the forgotten lunches.

When the train reached Warren, Ohio, about 5:00 p.m. that evening, friends of the sisters at St. Mary's Parish took the travelers to the convent for a quick dinner then drove them back to the station so that they could continue their journey.

The time traveling was spent praying, relaxing and watching the landscape change from the level plains of Indiana, Illinois, Iowa and Nebraska to the sandy deserts of Utah and Nevada, and finally to the orange groves and palm trees of Southern

---

19   The title "Mother" was not used by provincial superiors until 1936 when a revised edition of the Constitutions was issued. However, for the sake of clarity, the title of "Mother" is given to Sister Mary Evarista throughout this account.
Mother Mary Evarista (Anna Barbara Harks) entered the Sisters of Notre Dame in 1887 in Cleveland, Ohio. She served as District Superior in Covington, Kentucky (1914-1917), Superior of all the Sisters of Notre Dame in the United States (1918-1924) and Provincial Superior in Cleveland, until her death in 1943.
20   Cited in Wittenburg, House, 6. ASNDTO.

California. On Saturday, August 30th the Feast of St. Rose of Lima, the train pulled into the Union Pacific Station at First and Mission Streets in Los Angeles. The little group of pioneers separated immediately. Sister Mary Balbina, Sister Mary Alice, Sister Mary Sirana, Sister Mary Clarissa and Sister Mary Blanche took a taxi to Watts; while Father Pierse and Mr. Emmerick drove the remaining six sisters down bumpy, unpaved Slauson Avenue to Huntington Park.

Huntington Park, "The City of Perfect Balance"

Located five miles southeast of downtown Los Angeles, the region that eventually became Huntington Park, was originally made up of ranches, farmland and orchards. But early in the twentieth century all that had changed. Developers A. L. Burbank and E. V. Baker persuaded Henry E. Huntington to extend his Pacific Electric Railway into the neighborhood. For a five cent fare, the "Los Angeles Railway [provided] 5 and 10 minute service to all points in Los Angeles"[21] thereby making it possible for one to work in downtown Los Angeles yet live beyond the city limits where land was cheaper.

At the same time, due to its location along the Alameda Corridor – a strip of land which connected downtown Los Angeles with the ports of Los Angeles and Long Beach – Huntington Park was becoming the center of a rapidly expanding industrial and commercial area. Factories within the city limits and in the adjacent district produced steel, iron, automobile supplies, furniture, heavy hardware, and paint as well as other products. Surrounding the city were large poultry farms. Fertile orchards supplied citrus fruits to the area.

By the mid-1920s, Huntington Park had a predominantly middle class population of 12,500 individuals, all of whom were Caucasian. An article in the Los Angeles *Times,* dated 1924, described the residents of the community as "home-

---

21   Huntington Park, California: The City of Perfect Balance, 1923, n.p. History and Genealogy Department, Richard J. Riordan Central Library, Los Angeles.

loving, public-spirited citizens, a large per cent owning their own homes."[22]

St. Matthias Parish

St. Matthias Convent, 1924

The parish of St. Matthias was already eleven years old when the first Sisters of Notre Dame arrived in California. Mass had been celebrated in private homes in the neighborhood until 1913 when the parish was formally erected and a small frame church built at the corner of Seville Street and Belgrave Avenue. When Reverend Mother Mary Cecilia visited St. Matthias Parish in March 1924, the convent was nearly completed. Construction of a four-classroom school was scheduled to begin shortly and would be, Father Pierse promised, "ready in September."[23]

22   "At the City's Gates," January 1, 1924. *Los Angeles Times*, F3. History and Genealogy Department, Richard J. Riordan Central Library, Los Angeles.
23   Letter, May 1924. ASNDC.

Upon their arrival, the sisters were welcomed with a special dinner prepared by several women from the parish. Two days later, on Monday, September 1, 1924, Bishop Cantwell formally blessed both the school and convent.

The sisters spent the next two weeks preparing for school. Sister Mary Bernard, however, found time to share her first impressions of Southern California in a letter to the community in Cleveland written shortly after their arrival:

> The houses here are really like doll houses. They are not like the bungalows in the East, they are much smaller. The architecture is so varied that one cannot easily find two of the exact same style. Each little home is made most picturesque by the number of beautiful palms, vines and flowers of all kinds....Although the trees look as if they needed a thorough washing, the lawns are kept fresh and green by means of irrigation. This is arranged by water pipes laid beneath the sod with small openings here and there so that when the water is turned on, the entire lawn is covered with small fountains.
>
> You really ought to see the traffic,--and the way in which one auto tries to pass another. In Cleveland, the autos on the avenues have the privilege of passing, while those on the side streets must politely wait, but here it is not so,--whoever can make it, tries to outdo the other man and thus one is almost afraid of collisions at each crossing.
>
> Talking about traffic and streets, well you surely won't believe it.... but we saw here in Los Angeles, while coming from the depot,--on one of the main streets, the big locomotive with its train of freight and other cars. It has a track for itself, almost in the middle of the street....There seems to be a lack of that system or regularity which is common in our eastern cities. I wish that I could remember the variety of shops and stores, mills and places of manufacture, all confused and scattered here and there. Some have their wares

hanging on the outside,--while others have open places like market stalls, with tinware and other articles
on display. The dark-faced Mexicans passing up and
down and girls with Japanese parasols made us feel
very much like foreign missionaries.

Here in Huntington Park it is very much the same as
in the East, except that the prices are very high. Imagine
someone asking 5 cents for three sheets of tissue pa-
per, or 7 cents for a yard of baby ribbon, 1/4 inch wide.
Articles are surely at least twice as expensive as they are
at home. It must be because there are so few factories
and all seems to be bought in the East, and sold here at
higher prices in consequence.[24]

Sister Mary Bernard's letter also contained a bit of advice:

If anyone of you…is ever to prepare to come to
California, be sure to be 'gitten yourslif' well posted
in the Irish brogue. We speak about 'Little Italy' in
Cleveland, -- well this is surely 'Little Ireland.' You
never heard so much of it in all your life, -- sure you
didn't. We will be talking that way I'm afraid myself,-
-sure 'tis that.[25]

Classes began for 215 children on September 15th.
Sister Mary Isabel taught grades one and two; Sister Mary
Walburge, three and four; and Sister Mary Ellen, five and
six. Originally Sister Mary Bernard was to be a non-teach-
ing principal. Sister, however, felt sorry for the older children and decided to teach the seventh and eighth grades
herself. At the same time, Sister Mary Hildegarde began
music lessons. Eventually a sewing class for older girls, directed by Sister Mary Amandis, was added.

---

24   [Sister Mary Bernard Flury, S.N.D.], Letter to Sister Superior [Mary Evarista
Harks] et al., September 1924. ASNDC.
25   Ibid.

Watts, California

Once part of a large Spanish land grant, the area known as Watts was basically a farming region until 1907 when the Pacific Electric Railroad selected it as the site for a train station and ignited a fever of subdivision. The streetcar line gave the residents direct access to downtown Los Angeles and to jobs available there. Furthermore land in Watts itself was cheap. Consequently it was possible for a family to own "a house and a garden and pigs and chickens, and a fruit tree"[26] at almost no cost. Thus, Watts became essentially a residential community.

The population was diverse. Caucasian Americans – mostly Germans and Scots -- settled in the southwest. Hispanics, trying to avoid conscription into the Mexican army, found work on the railroad and built homes in the same area. A small number of African-Americans, migrating from the south, took jobs on the railroad serving as Pullman car porters, carpenters and blacksmiths. This group tended to settle in the southeast below 103rd Street. A minority of Japanese also maintained truck gardens in the neighborhood.

---

26   Jane Birnbaum, "Watts redevelopment has a history to build on," <u>Los Angeles Herald</u> <u>Examiner</u>, July 29, 1989, A3. History and Genealogy Department, Richard J. Riordan Central Library, Los Angeles.

St. Lawrence of Brindisi Parish

St. Lawrence Brindisi Parish

The Franciscan Capuchin Order had been active on the west coast since 1910 when Father Luke Sheehan, O.F.M. Cap. arrived in Oregon. In 1922, the opportunity to extend their ministry to Southern California arose when Bishop Cantwell sent a petition to the superiors of the Order asking them to establish a foundation in his diocese. The site offered to them was Holy Redeemer Parish in Watts, erected by the Right Reverend Thomas J. Conaty in 1908. The Provincial Chapter accepted the Bishop's request on the condition that the name of the parish was changed to St. Lawrence of Brindisi, a 17th century Capuchin saint.

Father Joseph Fenelon, O.F.M., Cap.[27] had been pastor of the new foundation for a little more than a year when he met Sister

---

27   A native of County Carlow, Ireland, Father Joseph Fenelon, O.F.M. Cap. entered the order in 1892 and was ordained to the priesthood in 1901. Father Joseph came to the United States in 1918 and served as pastor of St. Lawrence of Brindisi Parish (1922-1929) and St. Francis of Assisi Parish (1923-1935). He subsequently ministered first in

Mary Bernard and Sister Mary Josita at St. Anthony Church in Long Beach and made up his mind to ask Mother Mary Cecilia if the Sisters of Notre Dame would staff his newly built school.

For the sisters at St. Lawrence of Brindisi Parish the first days were memorable ones as well. Although the school building was a large, eight-grade structure, Father Joseph could only afford to equip four classrooms. Anticipating a maximum enrollment of 160 pupils, he had arranged forty desks in each room. The number of children who actually registered on the first day exceeded the pastor's expectations, so more desks had to be crowded into each classroom. The lower grades especially were full, but this did not daunt the sisters, particularly Sister Mary Clarissa, who taught over seventy first and second graders nearly all year.

The missionary character of their ministry was vividly brought home to the sisters when they knelt behind the children at Mass the following day. "The children...seemed to be of all nations and colors," the Annals noted.[28] Sister Mary Balbina described the scene in a letter to Mother Mary Evarista. "You should have seen especially the little ones...Some came bare-footed, while others wore overalls. Many of the children were so dark that for the time being we thought we were in Africa."[29]

Oregon and later in Delaware. Father Fenelon died on April 20, 1963 at Holy Trinity Monastery in Ireland where he had been living since his retirement in 1947.
28   [Sister Mary Sirana Kirchner], Annals, St. Lawrence of Brindisi Convent: 1925-1926, 2-3. ASNDTO. Cited hereinafter as Annals, St. Lawrence. ASNDTO.
29   [Sister Mary Balbina Hagedorn], Letter to Sister Superior [Mary Evarista Harks] et al., September 7, 1924. ASNDC.

"This is what we're here for!"

St. Lawrence Convent

Seventy-five years later it is easy to ignore the challenges these eleven women faced during their first years in California. One of these was separation from the rest of the community in Ohio. In the 1920s, the sisters' contacts with their relatives were extremely restricted. Consequently, the sense of family among the sisters was both tangible and treasured. Because personal correspondence between individual sisters was not permitted, the sisters in California looked forward to visits by superiors and sisters from Cleveland. Community get-togethers at Christmas, Easter and during the summer vacation were eagerly anticipated.

Originally the sisters had expected to make their annual retreat in Cleveland. However, Reverend Mother Mary Cecilia decided they should remain in California. Therefore, in June 1925, Sister Mary Hildegarde composed a letter from the sisters at St. Matthias to the sisters at St. Lawrence inviting them to spend their summer vacation in Huntington Park.[30] Although the tone of the letter is humorous, it masks a keen sense of disappointment that they were unable to return to Ohio.

Another challenge which the sisters in California faced was the conditions under which they were called upon to teach. When the sisters arrived in late August, neither of the two schools was ready to open. Although the classrooms at both St. Matthias and St. Lawrence of Brindisi were furnished, no books or supplies had been ordered. Since the sisters were not familiar with local vendors, they had to deal with companies in the mid-west, an awkward and time-consuming situation. Furthermore, since the Office of Superintendent of Schools[31] had not yet adopted standardized application forms, absence records or permanent record cards, the sisters had to either improvise or adapt the materials they had used in Ohio.

Teaching itself was especially challenging at St. Lawrence of Brindisi. Not only were the classrooms crowded but attendance was sporadic. Some children stopped coming when their parents could no longer afford the tuition. Other families waited until the fruit-picking season on the nearby ranches was over and they had saved enough money to pay the necessary fees, then enrolled their children, usually one or two months late. Still others left before the fifth grade in order to take advantage of

---

30   [Sister Mary Hildegarde Delahanty], Letter to "Dearly Beloved Sisters in our Foreign Missions!!!," St. Anthony's Day, 1925. ASNDC.
31   Bishop John J. Cantwell had established the Office of Superintendent of Schools in 1920 in order to improve and coordinate various educational programs throughout his diocese.

the vocational training programs offered by the public schools. Consequently the sisters found it difficult to keep their classes progressing at a reasonable pace.

Another challenge in these first years was Mother Mary Evarista's attitude toward the foundations in California. The sisters' presence at both St. Matthias and St. Lawrence of Brindisi was largely the result of Reverend Mother Mary Cecilia's efforts. She herself had conducted the negotiations with the hierarchy and viewed foundations in California not only as a means of spreading the Congregation's educational ministry to the west coast but as a source of future vocations as well.[32] For this reason Reverend Mother Mary Cecilia was particularly eager to accept the school in St. Gregory Nazianzen Parish in Los Angeles. Since it was located in a residential area, she felt it would provide more stability. "In most other places, you could see only apartment houses, and the population is continually changing." Moreover, the convent was within walking distance of Catholic Girls High School which she envisioned future aspirants could attend.[33]

Reverend Mother Mary Cecilia, however, died in April 1925, and Mother Mary Evarista did not necessarily share her sentiments. Reverend Mother Mary Cecilia had left the decision about accepting the school in St. Gregory Nazianzen Parish as well as expanding the sisters' ministry into the Diocese of San Bernardino up to her, neither of which she did. Although Mother Mary Evarista had provided sisters to staff the two schools, she had never been enthusiastic about the endeavor.[34] She felt that the eleven sisters were badly needed in the schools in Ohio.

Moreover, Los Angeles was far away from the rest of the community, a fact which made communication difficult. Furthermore, Hollywood, which in the 1920s was synonymous with Southern California, had a lurid reputation. Lastly, there was always the possibility of earthquakes and, at least in Mother Mary Evarista's mind, the threat of Indians.

---

32   Letter, February 21, 1925. ASNDC.
33   Ibid.
34   Ibid.

During the first years, there was a very real possibility that Mother Mary Evarista might close the California houses. In fact, when she visited Los Angeles for the first time in the autumn of 1924, she was seriously considering taking the sisters back to Cleveland with her. She had informed Bishop Cantwell of her intention and promised to notify him if she decided to recall the sisters to Ohio. Only His Excellency's admonition to "write only 'love notes'" [good news] had persuaded her not to do so.

Mother Mary Evarista's indecision was still apparent the following summer (1925) when the sisters received no appointments. Retreat opened and closed at St. Matthias with no word from the superiors in Ohio. In the end, the sisters simply returned to their same duties and affiliations. This state of affairs lasted until 1928, when Mother Mary Evarista sent Sister Mary Flavia Lübke and Sister Mary Cyrene Schreiner to replace Sister Mary Ellen and Sister Mary Alice whom she recalled to Cleveland. It was not until 1941 when Mother Mary Evarista herself accepted St. Helen School in South Gate that the permanence of the California foundation was assured.[35]

Although challenges such as these – distance from the rest of the community, teaching conditions and the attitude of the superiors – might be regarded as "hardships," the first sisters in California never considered them so. Such difficulties were merely part of the mission to which they had been called. Open to the Spirit, mindful of God's goodness and trusting in his provident care, there was apparently nothing to which these eleven women would say "no." It was always "How Good is the Good God" and "That's what we're here for."

---

35   During the period from 1928 – 1942, the sisters had accepted two additional schools – St. Rose of Lima in Maywood (1930) and St. Francis of Assisi in Los Angeles. (1938). Permission to do so, however, had come directly from Reverend Mother Mary Antonie.

Chapter Two

Mother Julie's Work

*St. Lawrence First Communion, 1925 – Sisters L-R, Sr. Mary Sirana
Kirchner, Sr. Mary Blanche Wolf, Sr. Mary Balbina Hagedorn,
Sr. Mary Hildegard Delahanty, Sr. Mary Isabel Lang*

Religious education has always been an essential component of
the Congregation's apostolate. Therefore, it is not surprising
that it quickly became an integral part of the sisters' ministry in
both Huntington Park and Watts.

In February 1925, just six months after their arrival, Sister Mary Hildegarde and Sister Mary Isabel began catechism classes on Saturdays and Sundays for the children in the nearby parish of St. Rose of Lima, Maywood,[36] first in a neighbor's back yard and later in the sacristy of the church. By 1927, the sisters were also involved in the religious education program in their own parish of St. Matthias. By the end of that year, approximately 200 children from both parishes were receiving religious instruction from the sisters.

At St. Lawrence of Brindisi the story was much the same. School had scarcely begun when the sisters realized that many of the older students had not made their First Holy Communion. Therefore, a special after-school class was quickly organized in order to prepare them to receive the Sacrament. At the same time, Father Laurence O'Connor, pastor of Our Lady of Victory Parish in Compton, asked the sisters to begin religious instruction in his parish, so, each Sunday Sister Mary Balbina and Sister Mary Sirana made the trip to Compton to prepare the children to receive the sacraments. The sisters, however, had to discontinue this work in October of the following year, 1925, in order to take over the public school instruction in their own parish. At the same time, the sisters became involved in the work of the newly organized Confraternity of Christian Doctrine.

The Confraternity of Christian Doctrine

The overthrow of Mexican dictator Porfirio Diaz by Francisco Madero in 1911 had brought an end to the period of relative calm which the Catholic Church had enjoyed in that country. Almost immediately, signs of hostility against the Church became apparent. By the 1920s religious persecution was widespread. Churches were secularized and foreign-born priests and

---

36   Father Thomas Stack, the pastor of St. Rose of Lima Parish had also asked for sisters for his school. But neither Reverend Mother Mary Cecilia nor Mother Mary Evarista felt they could spare any sisters at the time, so they suggested that the sisters at St. Matthias begin catechism classes at St. Rose of Lima so that the children of the parish would receive some form of religious instruction.

religious expelled. As a result, many Mexican people, in search of the human rights denied by their own government, sought refuge in Southern California. "By 1923 an estimated 150,000 exiles were residing in Los Angeles County alone. In the two-year period between 1925 and 1926, another 80,000 found their way into Southern California."[37]

The presence of such large numbers of immigrants presented a challenge to Bishop Cantwell and to the Church of Los Angeles since many of the people pouring into Southern California lacked any formal religious education and training. An outgrowth of Cantwell's concern was the formal establishment of the Confraternity of Christian Doctrine (C.C.D.) in 1923, an organization whose goal was to provide an expanded program of religious education among the Mexican immigrants.[38]

The Confraternity of Christian Doctrine of Los Angeles had actually had its beginning five years earlier through the efforts of a young public school teacher, Verona Spellmire. Hours of volunteer work in one of the city's settlement houses as well as her own experiences in the classroom had shown her how little knowledge of their Catholic faith these immigrants had. In 1918, through an article in <u>Our Sunday Visitor</u>, Spellmire had learned of the work of the Missionary Confraternity in Pittsburgh.[39] This organization, she had concluded, offered a way to combat the ignorance she had encountered among the Mexican people in Los Angeles. The following summer, 1919, Spellmire and ten of her women friends had organized a series

37   Grebler, Leo. "Mexican Immigration in the United States: The Record and its Implications," 1965.

38   Rev. Dennis J. Burke, "The History of the Confraternity of Christian Doctrine in the Diocese of Los Angeles, 1922-1936," Dissertation, Catholic University of America, Washington, D.C. AALA.

39   The Confraternity of Christian Doctrine, founded in Rome in 1560 by Marco de Sadis-Cusani, had been introduced in the United States following the Second Plenary Council of Baltimore (1866) in three dioceses: New York (1902), Pittsburgh (1907) and Brooklyn (1921). In Pittsburgh the Confraternity of Christian Doctrine was essentially based in the city, The Missionary Confraternity of Christian Doctrine established the following year, provided religious instruction to children in rural areas of the diocese.

of catechetical classes at Simon's Brickyard, a Mexican *colonia* east of Los Angeles.

Over the next three years, Spellmire's enthusiasm for the Confraternity had continued to grow. At the same time she had begun looking for a way to establish a similar diocesan-wide organization in Los Angeles. Early in 1922, she had shared her ideas with Reverend Robert E. Lucey, the new Director of Catholic Charities. Lucey, in turn, had presented Spellmire's proposal to Bishop Cantwell. The Bishop had readily endorsed the plan especially since it provided a solution to his own concern for the Mexican people in his diocese. Shortly afterwards, in April 1922, following a house-to-house visitation, Spellmire and a group of women and men volunteers had organized the first religious education class at St. Anthony's Mission in East Los Angeles.

The group, however, had quickly realized that their work needed a more definite organizational structure if it was to expand. Therefore, at a meeting held at Our Lady of Guadalupe Church [now Immaculate Conception Church, on James M. Wood Boulevard] on April 16, 1923, Spellmire had presented for adoption a short constitution based on that of the Missionary Confraternity in Pittsburgh. Among other things, the document called for the establishment of "centers" for religious instruction in neighborhoods where they were needed. Two such centers, directed by volunteers from Holy Cross Parish in South Los Angeles assisted by the Sisters of Notre Dame, had been located in St. Lawrence of Brindisi Parish.

It quickly became apparent, however, that these two centers were not sufficient for the estimated 1,300 Catholic children who belonged to the parish but attended public schools. In 1926, eight additional centers were established in the parish. Center #4 was located at St. Lawrence of Brindisi School and was under the direction of the sisters. Classes opened on October 30th for 38 students. But the enrollment increased steadily. The <u>Annals</u> noted: "From December till May [1926-1927] we had an average attendance of 160 children on Saturdays." [40]

---

40   <u>Annals</u>, St. Lawrence of Brindisi Convent: 1924-1931, 24-25. ASNDTO.

The sisters' involvement in the work of the Confraternity of Christian Doctrine took on another dimension three years later, in 1929, when they added Religious Vacation Schools to their catechetical ministry. The idea of Religious Vacation Schools had been piloted in six parishes in Los Angeles in the summer of 1928. The project had been so successful that the following year, Bishop Cantwell asked each of the religious communities in his diocese to contribute two teachers to the summer program so that it could be expanded to all the parishes in the diocese. At St. Lawrence of Brindisi, Sister Mary Balbina, Sister Mary Flavia and Sister Mary Sirana taught catechism, Bible History and singing as well as some craftwork which correlated with the day's lesson.

Such religious instruction was not easy, for the sisters had to contend with poverty, parental indifference and ignorance. "There are boys and girls at the ages of thirteen, fourteen and fifteen years who do not know the Lord's Prayer," the Annals stated.

> Some ignorant parents take their children to confession and Holy Communion without any preparation whatsoever. Many of these people do not think of attending Holy Mass on Sundays. But when they have a Baptism the whole family turns out. Some seem to be under the impression that after their First Holy Communion they are dispensed from hearing mass on Sundays.[41]

These difficulties, however, were accepted as simply part of their ministry. Sister Mary Sirana expressed the view shared by all the sisters: "We have good reason to exclaim with our holy foundress: 'My God, how good Thou art to have sent us to these little ones.'"[42]

The sisters' efforts bore fruit in many tangible ways. Anxious to expand the Congregation's ministry in Southern California, Sister Mary Bernard encouraged the sisters to accept a pastor's invitation to direct the religious education program in his parish.

---

41   Ibid. 12-13.
42   Ibid.

She was convinced that when he ultimately opened a school, he would ask for Sisters of Notre Dame to staff it.

Sister Mary Bernard's assumption proved to be accurate since the growth of the sisters' educational ministry during the next fifteen years, 1930 – 1945, was a direct result of the sisters' catechetical instruction in St. Rose of Lima, St. Helen and St. Leo parishes.

St. Rose of Lima School, Maywood

Although the parish of St. Rose of Lima in Maywood had been erected in 1922, it was not until the spring of 1929 that Father John Dignam, the fourth pastor, broke ground for a parochial school. Since he was familiar with the Sisters of Notre Dame through the community's involvement in the parish's religious education program,[43] Father Dignam took advantage of Reverend Mother Mary Antonie's presence in Los Angeles to request sisters for his school. On September 2, 1930, St. Rose of Lima School opened its doors to 185 eager students.

St. Helen School, South Gate

Both St. Helen School in South Gate and St. Leo School in Watts followed a similar pattern. St. Helen Parish had been erected in 1931 following a division of the parish of St. Matthias. Since September 1933, the sisters at St. Matthias had taught religious education classes as well as conducted a Vacation School for the children of the new parish. When the pastor, Father Thomas O'Donnell, decided to open a school, he asked the Sisters of Notre Dame to staff it. Mother Mary Evarista promised eight sisters for September 1941.

Although Father O'Donnell had broken ground for the school early in 1941, the restrictions imposed by World War II

---

43   Cf. Chapter 2, p. 1, fn. 1. Father John Dignam succeeded Father Thomas Stack as pastor in 1926 and served the parish until his death in 1941.

had seriously hampered construction. By the middle of July the school was still a shell and the sisters' convent not ready for occupancy.[44] At first, St. Helen's faculty found temporary accommodations at the other Notre Dame convents in the area. Toward the end of August, Sister Mary Dolores Grauel, principal and superior at St. Rose of Lima, Maywood, offered the sisters use of the faculty room on the second floor of the school, which they quickly transformed into a dormitory-study hall. There the sisters assigned to St. Helen tried to prepare for school while at the same time shuttling back and forth to South Gate each Sunday in order to conduct religious education classes for the children in the parish. Finally on September 24, 1941 the sisters were able to move into their new home.

Although the school building itself was still unfinished, the sisters were determined to begin classes on September 29, 1941 as planned. This they did in a variety of locations – on the cement driveway next to the convent, in the church itself and in the convent yard.[45] These conditions lasted until early December when the building was finally ready for occupancy and the sisters could conduct their classes in a more conventional academic setting.

St. Leo School, Watts

The sisters had been actively involved in religious education in the area which eventually became St. Leo Parish since 1926, when Sister Mary Balbina and Sister Mary Sirana had directed the religious education program at Confraternity of Christian Doctrine Center #3 in the El Jardin district in South Los Angeles.

The following year, 1927, several Mexican families purchased two lots on El Jardin Avenue and moved a small house on to the property which they renovated as a convent. They also built a small chapel at the rear of the convent which they dedicated to

---

44   Rev. Terrence O'Donnell, Letter to Mother Mary Evarista, July 16, 1941. ASNDC.

45   The Sisters of St. Helen's, Letter to Mother Mary Evarista et al., November, 1941. ASNDC. Cited hereinafter as Letter, November 1941, ASNDC.

Our Lady of the Angels. Although a group of Sisters of Perpetual Adoration from Mexico had moved into the convent and begun sewing classes for the women of the neighborhood, they were not fluent in English. Consequently, the sisters from St. Lawrence of Brindisi had continued to give religious instruction on Saturdays in El Jardin. In 1933, however, these classes were discontinued. Between 1933 and 1938, the sisters had very little contact with the people of the El Jardin District with the exception of a small group of African-American girls who had attended St. Lawrence of Brindisi School.

In 1938, Father Leandro Arias, pastor at Our Lady of the Angels Parish, asked the sisters to resume religious instruction in El Jardin. As a result, in November, three sisters from St. Lawrence of Brindisi began catechism classes on Wednesday afternoons for the children in the neighborhood. As soon as they met the children, the sisters realized that once again they had been called to do Mother Julie's work. The <u>Annals</u> of St. Lawrence of Brindisi noted:

The children are dirty and neglected, and were at first very unruly, not used to silence and order in the class room, and of course very ignorant in religious matters.[46]

The next summer, 1939, Our Lady of the Angels Parish was added to the list of Vacation Schools conducted by the Sisters of Notre Dame.

Despite the establishment of Our Lady of the Angels Chapel in the area in 1927, distance had continued to be a problem for families living north of Imperial Highway. Consequently, in 1933, a group of African-American families built a small church on 113th Street and placed it under the patronage of St. Leo. In 1942, Father John McNulty, pastor at St. Leo, asked the sisters at St. Lawrence of Brindisi to take over the Saturday catechism classes, attend Mass with the children on Sunday and conduct a Vacation School. Since the sisters were already involved in a similar work in nearby El Jardin as well as in their own parish,

---

46   <u>Annals</u>, St. Lawrence of Brindisi Convent: 1938-1939. ASNDTO.

they had to refuse. Father McNulty then turned to the sisters at St. Matthias.

During the next two years, 1942-1944, two sisters made the trip from Huntington Park to El Jardin each Saturday and Sunday morning during the school year. During the summer, sisters from St. Lawrence of Brindisi and St. Helen's convents traveled to Watts in order to conduct a Vacation School in St. Leo Parish.

Father McNulty, however, did not feel that this arrangement adequately met the children's spiritual needs, particularly those of the older boys and girls. Consequently, he asked now *Archbishop* Cantwell[47] for permission to open a parochial school. Rather than begin a building program at a time when wartime restrictions were seriously limiting construction, Archbishop Cantwell suggested that Father McNulty use the empty building on El Jardin Avenue, across from Our Lady of the Angels Church, for his school. This, the Archbishop had pointed out, would give the children of both neighborhoods the opportunity for a Catholic education.

Father McNulty agreed and tentatively set September 1944 for the opening of St. Leo School. In December 1943, Father presented his request for sisters to the recently elected provincial superior, Mother Mary Vera[48] who forwarded the letter to Reverend Mother Mary Antonie, then in Brazil. Reverend Mother Mary Antonie's affirmative reply reached Cleveland shortly after Christmas[49] so Mother Mary Vera's 1944 Vacation Letter contained the names of the five sisters who would conduct the Vacation Schools at St. Leo and Our Lady of the Angels parishes and supervise the preparations for the opening of St.

---

47   The Right Reverend John J. Cantwell was created an archbishop in December 1936 when the four Southern California counties of Santa Barbara, Ventura, Los Angeles and Orange became the Archdiocese of Los Angeles.

48   Mother Mary Vera (Anna Angela Niess) had succeeded Mother Mary Evarista as Provincial Superior in July 1943. She had entered the Sisters of Notre Dame in Cleveland, Ohio in 1917; was appointed Provincial Superior in Cleveland in 1943 and elected fifth Superior General of the Sisters of Notre Dame in 1946. Reverend Mother Mary Vera died in April 1962.

49   [Mother Mary Antonie Sommer], Telegram to Mother Vera Niess, No date. ASNDC.

Leo School in September. This latter assignment proved to be a formidable task.

Although the building which Archbishop Cantwell had suggested Father McNulty use for his school had been erected in 1932, Our Lady of the Angels Parish had been unable to maintain it. As a result, it had been used for occasional gatherings and ultimately left unoccupied. After the 1933 Long Beach Earthquake, the Willowbrook School District had rented the building and their students had caused serious damage. The adjacent convent, which had been erected at the same time as the school, had suffered similar neglect. By 1944, both buildings needed major repairs before they could be used again. Throughout the summer months, the sisters, together with volunteers from the neighborhood, cleaned and scrubbed the convent while workmen replaced cracked blackboards, corrected faulty electrical wiring, and repaired broken windows in the school, and, at the same time, gave both buildings a fresh coat of paint. [50]

The weeks before classes began were crowded with cleaning and arranging classrooms and taking registration. By the opening of school, September 5, 1944, the enrollment had reached 227 children of Hispanic and African-American ancestry with two Irish and one French family for variety. The first day of classes was made even more interesting for the sisters as they tried to twist their tongues around such musical names as Jesusita, Soledad, Natividad, Arzlee, Phomie and Ivory.

St. Francis of Assisi School, Los Angeles

The last affiliation opened during this period, 1930-1945, at St. Francis of Assisi Parish did not support Sister Mary Bernard's belief that the sisters' involvement in the parish's religious education program would lead to the pastor's asking the community

---

50   The Archives of the Sisters of Notre Dame, Chardon, Ohio contain a series of letters from the sisters at St. Leo Convent to Mother Mary Vera in Cleveland which describe in detail the conditions that the sisters faced that first summer. Letters to Mother Mary Vera , June 25, 1944, July 2, 1944, July 11, 1944, July 13, 1944 and July 24, 1944. ASNDC.

to staff his school. Still, the same willingness to respond to the needs of the Church, commitment to their ministry and trust in God's provident care which had characterized the sisters' work elsewhere led to the opening of the fourth foundation in Southern California, St. Francis of Assisi School.[51]

From the community's first days at St. Lawrence of Brindisi Parish, the pastors, first Father Joseph Fenelon, O.F.M. Cap., and later his successor, Father Stephen Murtagh, O.F.M. Cap.,[52] had been very solicitous for the sisters' needs. Consequently, the sisters felt a deep regret when they learned that Father Stephen had been transferred to St. Francis of Assisi Parish in Hollywood.

St. Francis of Assisi was not a new parish. Established as a diocesan parish in 1920 to care for the spiritual needs of the Irish and German families in the area, the parish had been transferred to the Paulist Fathers in 1925. The community had staffed it until 1929 at which time it had been turned over to the Capuchin Franciscans of the Irish Province.

None of Father Murtagh's predecessors at St. Francis had felt the need for a parish school. At St. Lawrence of Brindisi Parish, however, Father Stephen had seen the important role that a parochial school could play in parish life. Therefore, he was determined to open a school at St. Francis of Assisi as soon as possible

By Easter, 1938, Father Stephen had acquired property on Golden Gate Avenue next to the rectory. During the summer, he and a crew of carpenters began renovating a two-story building which had formerly served as the first church, next as the rectory and finally as the parish hall. The lower floor was divided into two classrooms: one for grades five and six, the other for grades seven and eight. The second story was arranged as the sisters'

---

51   St. Matthias, Huntington Park, and St. Lawrence of Brindisi, Watts, were established in 1924; St. Rose of Lima, Maywood, in 1930 and St. Francis of Assisi, Los Angeles, in 1938.

52   Father Stephen Murtagh, O.F.M., Cap., a native of County Longford, Ireland, was ordained a priest as a member of the Capuchin order in 1918. Appointed pastor of St. Lawrence of Brindisi Parish in 1925, he served the people of the neighborhood until 1937. In that year he was named pastor of St. Francis of Assisi Parish in Los Angeles as well as provincial of the Capuchin order.

living quarters. Grades one to four were located in a small bungalow nearby.[53]

Father Stephen was familiar with the charism and educational heritage of the Congregation through his years at St. Lawrence of Brindisi Parish and so he asked Reverend Mother Mary Antonie for Sisters of Notre Dame for his school. Reverend Mother Mary Antonie's telegram arrived on June 13, 1938 – "Accept St. Francis of Assisi."[54] Coincidently, it was the feast of St. Anthony under whose patronage the matter had been placed.

Ninety-two students reported for school on the first day, September 6, 1939. By November, the enrollment had risen to 115 pupils. "We were very close to the children in those days," Sister Mary Louise Wanamaker recalled. "We often shared their recesses and, since the school had no electric bell system, summoned the children to class by standing in the yard and ringing a hand bell."[55] At night the sisters could stand at the windows of their second floor convent and watch the lights come on at the Griffith Park Observatory and in the surrounding Hollywood Hills.

The year 1944 marked the twentieth anniversary of the sisters' arrival in Southern California. The number of sisters stationed on the west coast had risen from eleven to forty-eight; the number of schools from two to six. In addition to formal classroom instruction the sisters were involved in religious education programs and Vacation Schools in their own and neighboring parishes.

Besides numbers, however, the sisters in California had forged a unique spirit – one of openness to the Spirit, commitment to their ministry in California and deep loyalty to the Congregation. This achievement was due, in no small measure, to Sister Mary Bernard.

53   [Sisters at St. Francis of Assisi], Letter, September 1938. ASNDC. Cited hereinafter as Letter, September 1938. ASNDC.
54   Annals, St. Francis of Assisi Convent, 1938-1939. ASNDTO.
55   Sister Mary Louise Wanamaker, S.N.D., Personal Conversation, 1972. Cited in Wittenburg, House, 33. ASNDTO.

Nurturer of the Flame

Sr. Mary Bernard Flury, Golden Jubilee

Sister Mary Bernard (Rose Josephine Flury) was forty-two years old when Reverend Mother Mary Cecilia appointed her superior of the St. Matthias community in Huntington Park. She had entered the Congregation in Cleveland, Ohio in 1900 and had been a successful intermediate-grade teacher at St. Mary,

Sandusky; St. Ignatius, Toledo; and St. Paul, Norwalk, all in Ohio, before coming to California in 1924.

Although the assignment to open a school in the "West" meant leaving her family and friends, Sister Mary Bernard accepted her appointment with the same enthusiasm and generosity that had characterized her entire life. Her openness to the Spirit and trust in God's goodness enabled her to see the challenges of pioneering as simply part of his provident plan and she encouraged the sisters to do likewise.

Sister Mary Bernard was totally committed to the Congregation's ministry in California. Her greatest desire was to increase the number of foundations on the west coast. On July 4, 1926, Sister enthusiastically wrote to Mother Mary Evarista about Father Stack's request for sisters to staff St. Rose of Lima School in Maywood.

> Now won't that be fine, dear Sister Superior, then you'll have a better chance of changing us around – two houses is a couple, – three, a crowd. By the time 1927 comes around, you'll have some more sisters that need recuperation and they'll get "all fixed up" here, like the rest of us…Not as tho' you could find no other place to put them, I know that you can do that, but California is the best place to put them, nearest to heaven.[56]

Sister Mary Bernard herself would go to any lengths for California. She made sure that each sister continued her education and received the necessary degrees and credentials. This was accomplished with a great deal of sacrifice on Sister Mary Bernard's part since it meant finding someone to drive the sisters to and from Mount St. Mary's and Immaculate Heart College each Saturday and during the summer months.

The depth of Sister's commitment to California was particularly evident following the 1933 earthquakes. On March 10th, a severe quake had jolted the Long Beach area. Of the three

---

56   Sister Mary Bernard, Letter to Sister Superior Mary Evarista, July 4, 126. Cited in Sister Mary Joanne Wittenburg, S.N.D., "Women on Fire," Rosa Mystica Province, Summer 2001, n.p. ASNDTO. Cited hereinafter as Wittenburg, "Women," ASNDTO.

neighborhoods in which the sisters taught, – Watts, Maywood and Huntington Park – the latter was hit the hardest.

The parish plant at St. Matthias suffered major structural damage. The exterior of the auditorium had to be torn out and completely rebuilt as the iron beams had shifted. In the school all the classrooms had to be replastered, pictures reframed and statues replaced. The walls of the convent were reinforced with iron rods, then plastered and painted.

The repairs on St. Matthias School and convent were completed in time for the opening of classes in September 1933. Four weeks later, however, on October 2nd, another quake shook the area. This time the damage to the school was so extensive that the building inspectors tagged the entire structure as unsafe and ordered it torn down.

To Father Leo Murphy, the pastor, this news was devastating. Since the parish had just finished clearing the debt on a recent addition to the school and on the repairs necessitated by the March quake, he did not believe his parishioners could afford to undertake another building program. Consequently, Father Murphy decided to close St. Matthias School and to encourage the students to transfer to their neighborhood public school.

Sister Mary Bernard, however, was determined not to give up the school or to lose the children. After much prayerful reflection, especially to her favorite Infant of Prague, Sister decided to present the matter to Bishop Cantwell himself and to ask him to intervene on the students' behalf. Bishop Cantwell was very understanding and promised to call Father Murphy immediately. He ended his conversation with the pastor with the words: "'Leo, you do as your Bishop says. See the sisters this evening….and do anything to keep your children. God will bless you and your Bishop will help you.' As a result, Father Murphy said, he had no choice but to rebuild the school."[57]

Sister communicated her love and commitment to California to the sisters assigned to the west coast. Sister Mary Lenore Bott

---

57   Sister Mary St. Joseph Feickert, S.N.D., Letter to the author, 1973. Sister Mary St. Joseph had been Sister Mary Bernard's companion when she called upon Bishop Cantwell. Cited in Wittenburg, House, 29. ASNDTO.

remembered that Sister "had little patience with anyone who came and did not like it." According to Sister, "You hardly dared to be homesick."[58]

The sisters' separation from the rest of the Congregation in Ohio was a vital concern to Sister Mary Bernard. Sister wrote frequently to her superiors and kept the sisters up-to-date about affairs in the east. She never let the sisters in California forget that they were a vital part of the community in Cleveland.

For Sister Mary Bernard community was the keystone of a vibrant religious life. Trips to the mountains, picnics at the beach and especially community celebrations were among the means Sister Mary Bernard used to foster a sense of family among the sisters. The Fourth of July, a local superior's name day or a jubilee, and especially the anniversary of the sisters' arrival in California were occasions for what Sister Mary Bernard herself described as "dumb fun."

Sister Mary Joel Upmeier and Sister Mary Janette Dresman recalled that for each occasion the convent yard at St. Matthias was always festively decorated, and every effort was made to provide a wonderful time. Sister Mary Giovanne Vidoni commented, "Sister Mary Bernard knew that there was much work concerned with these affairs but she loved it when all [the sisters] were together in the family spirit."[59]

A spirit of mutual sharing and cooperation, honest enjoyment of each sister's presence as well as pride in their achievements are among Sister Mary Bernard's legacy to the sisters in California.

---

58   Sister Mary Lenore Bott, S.N.D., Personal Conversation, 1973. Cited in Wittenburg, "Women," n.p. ASNDTO.
59   Sister Mary Giovanne Vidoni, S.N.D., Letter to the author, 1975. Cited in Ibid, n.p.

Chapter Three

Notre Dame Convent

Notre Dame Academy, 1944

Of all the individuals who were part of the history of the Sisters of Notre Dame in California, perhaps no one left a more lasting mark than Reverend Mother Mary Vera Niess. As provincial superior in Cleveland (1943 - 1946), and then as Superior General of the Congregation itself (1946 - 1962), she, more than anyone else, shaped the growth and direction of the sisters' presence on the west coast.

As a young religious, Sister Mary Vera had lived for three and one half years at St. Matthias convent in Huntington Park while she earned her doctorate in education at the University of Southern California in Los Angeles. As a result, she understood from personal experience the hopes, joys and difficulties which the sisters faced as part of their ministry in California.

One of the hardships which the sisters felt was the distance from the rest of the community in the mid-west. In order to offset this feeling of separation and to instill a sense of "family" among the sisters assigned to California, Sister Mary Bernard had tried to bring them together as often as possible.

Although such get togethers helped to strengthen the family spirit, the sisters still wanted a place where they could all gather during the summer vacation, for the Christmas and Easter reunions and for the annual retreats. In 1932, they had started the California Fund into which they had poured the profits from countless raffles, music lessons, gifts and candied apple sales in the hope of accumulating enough money to purchase such a home. Despite such efforts, however, the sisters' dream of a central house had not materialized.

Consequently when Mother Mary Vera visited Southern California for the first time as provincial superior in March 1944, she was determined to find a site suitable for such a house and eventually for an academy and a novitiate. Mother Mary Vera visited several places in and around Los Angeles and finally found property in the Sunland-Tujunga area which seemed suitable. However, when she called upon Archbishop Cantwell in order to ask permission to purchase the property, events took an unexpected turn.

No sooner had Mother Mary Vera begun to describe the site, than the Archbishop suddenly interrupted: "That is not the place for you." Instead, he told Mother Mary Vera to contact Father William O'Shea, the pastor of St. Timothy Parish in West Los

Angeles[60], who had recently submitted the description of a two and one half acre tract on Overland Avenue which he wanted to purchase for a school.[61] The property together with a red brick colonial-style house was formerly part of the estate of Ferdinand R. Bain.

Rancho La Lomita

Ferdinand R. Bain, a native of Chatham, New York, and organizer and later Chairman of the Board of Southern Counties Gas Company, had come to California in 1911. In 1919, he had begun to purchase property in an area southwest of downtown Angeles, then known as Westwood Gardens. He planned to build a country home on the site and, at the same time, to pursue his interest in raising pure-bred livestock.

By 1924 Bain had acquired nearly 100 acres fronting on Overland Avenue. He had built a red brick colonial-style home on top of the Overland hill and surrounded the house with formal gardens and ornamental trees. He named his estate Rancho La Lomita or "Little Hill Ranch."

Bain had criss-crossed the land with fences and stocked the ranch with hogs, chickens, turkeys, sheep and cattle. The fields produced corn and alfalfa. There was also a model dairy from which milk and butter were sold to the large clubs and hotels in the area.

Bain's interest in agriculture was more than a hobby. During the 1920s he was recognized as a serious breeder of pure-bred Jersey cattle. Before building his own herd, he had visited

---

60   Father William T. O'Shea was born on June 2, 1902 in Clonakilty, County Cork, Ireland and ordained a priest there on June 18, 1928. After serving as assistant pastor in various parishes in the Diocese of Los Angeles-San Diego and the Archdiocese of Los Angeles, he was named pastor of St. Timothy Parish, in 1943, a position he held until his death in September 1963.

61   Annals, Notre Dame Academy. ASNDTO. A description of the visit with Archbishop Cantwell together with a history of the property itself and the opening pages of the Annals of Notre Dame Academy (October 1944 to December 1945) were written by Sister Mary Fortunata Horning, S.N.D. who, along with Sister Mary Bernard, had accompanied Mother Mary Vera to Archbishop Cantwell's office.

nearly all the Jersey breeders in the United States in order to determine which bloodlines would produce the utility and beauty he wanted. By 1925, he had a herd of nearly 300 head, many of which he had personally selected on his trips to Europe and to the Isle of Jersey. Robert T. Lyans reported in the Los Angeles *Times* that at Rancho La Lomita Bain had "developed a breeding establishment that ranks among the best in the country." Furthermore his herd of pure-breds "offers convincing evidence of his faith in [the] Channel Island breed, while the popular blood lines he has incorporated in his breeding reflect his unceasing effort to build up a herd of sterling worth not only as to production but as to outstanding breed type."[62] Lyans' opinion was reinforced by the fact that on the western show circuit, livestock from La Lomita repeatedly took home ribbons and grand championships.

Bain was extraordinarily proud of his herd. On more than one occasion, he had invited friends and other livestock breeders to dinner at his home and, at the end of the meal, thrown open the French doors of the dining room so that his guests could admire his prize cattle as his men drove them by.

The Depression, however, had affected Bain as it did many others. During the early 1930s he had leased part of his fields, keeping only the five acres surrounding the house for himself. This action, however, had not been sufficient. In the autumn of 1934 Bain had signed a trust deed and later a note with Rancho La Lomita as security. Four years later, in 1938 the bank had foreclosed, and issued a written Declaration of Default and Demand for Sale. On February 24, 1939 Rancho La Lomita had become the property of Security First National Bank.[63]

The acquisition of Rancho La Lomita, however, had posed somewhat of a problem for the bank since its officers were afraid that the property would be hard to resell. In their estimation, the lower portion of the tract was particularly unattractive. The

---

62   Robert T. Lyans, "A Great Southern California Jersey Establishment," Los Angeles Times, December 21, 1924, J9.

63   Wittenburg, House 47. ASNDTO.

Inspection Report had noted that, although the area to the west of Bain's estate, which was similar to this lower portion, had been subdivided, sales of the lots had been slow. The inspectors had also pointed out: "Unless the drainage problems [were] corrected, there [would] be very little interest in this section."[64] The house itself was considered an "over improvement," more suitable for a rest home or sanatorium. However, neither of these two predictions had come true.

At that time Paramount Pictures had been searching for a site on which to erect a $12 million dollar studio. In September 1939 Paramount had purchased Rancho La Lomita's 100 acres as well as an additional sixty acres which extended north from the ranch's northern boundary to Pico Boulevard. This acquisition had given the studio a 150-acre tract on which to build a studio. Paramount City, however, had never become a reality.

Paramount's plans for the development of the Overland property had moved ahead rapidly until December 7, 1941. Restrictions brought about by the United States' involvement in World War II coupled with the noise of planes taking off from the nearby Douglas Aircraft plant had ultimately made a motion picture studio in that location impossible. As a result, plans were abandoned and Paramount Pictures had eventually sold part of the land to the Overland Housing Company, which intended to build homes for defense workers on the site. By the time Mother Mary Vera saw the property in March 1944, most of the 150 acres had been subdivided and houses were already under construction. Only the two and one half acres surrounding the Bains' former home remained intact.

---

64   Inspection Report, Security Pacific Bank, Los Angeles, California, February 6, 1939. Cited in Ibid, 48.

"Overland"

Notre Dame Chapel

Although the property was in an ideal location for an academy, Mother Mary Vera did not feel the acreage was sufficient for the novitiate, juniorate and aspirant school which she envisioned for the site. Consequently, she returned to Cleveland without making a final decision.

Upon her return to California the following November, Mother Mary Vera once again visited properties in the Sunland-Tujunga, Arcadia, Azusa and Oxnard areas. In a letter to Archbishop Cantwell, dated November 8, 1944, Mother Mary Vera outlined her final decision about the Overland property; a decision she hoped to discuss with him during their meeting the following morning:

May we consummate the purchase within the next four months or so, of the property in West Los Angeles, and build there a modest elementary school? This school, with the home on the property, we can use then for the present for our yearly retreats and for the summer homecoming. The property is too small for building our novitiate, etc. No more adjacent property can be purchased.

May we purchase a ten-acre tract of land in Tujunga-Sunland, which is ideally located because of climate, to be used within the next several years for building our central home, novitiate, juniorate, and aspirant school. At that time, which is still in the future, perhaps you will also permit us to establish an elementary school in that district. This will help us to maintain ourselves.[65]

Archbishop Cantwell, however, was not in favor of the Sunland-Tujunga tract. He suggested that the sisters try to secure additional property next to the Overland site so that the community would have sufficient land on which to build the complex which Mother Mary Vera envisioned. Shortly afterward, seven lots on Clarkson Road-Selby Avenue side of the property became available for purchase.[66]

Once Father O'Shea had learned of Mother Mary Vera's interest in the Overland site, he did his utmost to help the community secure the property. Many of the difficulties which the sisters encountered were alleviated through his contacts within the motion picture industry, especially at 20th Century Fox Studios. The following excerpt from a letter, dated September 21, 1944, gives some indication of the obstacles, which he and Mr. Milton Pierson, the real estate agent and building contractor, encountered:

---

65   Mother Mary Vera [Niess], S.N.D., Letter to Most Reverend John J. Cantwell, D. D., November 8, 1944. AALA.
66   M. M. Vera [Niess], Letter to Most Reverend John J. Cantwell, December 29, 1944. AALA.

There is a great deal that I would like to tell you about the difficulties we have encountered during the last months, but that will keep until later. Three different companies have successively been on the verge of acquiring the entire tract on which the future convent is situated, and through each successive change, Mr. Pierson has kept constantly in touch with all concerned, working hopefully at all times, even when there seemed no hopes except your prayers.

Just now, and for weeks we are on a practically twenty-four hour watch to make sure we are leaving no stone unturned to secure the property for you, and we both feel that the prospect is very bright, and that if you and your Sisters continue your prayers we will be able to send you in the near future full information on the purchase so that you may turn it over to your legal advisor.[67]

Finally, on February 14, 1945, the Overland site was placed in escrow. Three and one half months later, on May 31, 1945, it became the property of the Sisters of Notre Dame.

Once the sisters had title to the property, cleaning and furnishing the house got underway.[68] Monday, June 25, 1945, was Homecoming Day. Since the convent could not accommodate all the sisters at the same time, they took turns vacationing at "Overland." Retreat began the next day, June 26, for the first group of eighteen sisters. On July 25, the two groups changed places. Following the close of the second retreat on August 22 and the sisters' departure three days later, only Sister Mary Loyole Gabal, Sister Mary Celestine Raetz and Sister Mary Gladys King remained at Overland in order to oversee the construction of the new elementary building and to prepare for the opening of school.

---

67   William T. O'Shea, Letter to Mother Mary Vera, S.N.D., September 21, 1944. ASNDC.

68   [Sisters in California], Letters to Mother Mary Vera et al., [Letter #1] June 28, 1945. ASNDTO. [Letter #2] Undated, ASNDC. [Letter #3], July 13, 1945. ASNDTO, [Letter #4], Undated, ASNDC.

That autumn, Mother Mary Vera, together with her two companions, Sister Mary Jeanita Fitz and Sister Mary Marguerite McArdle, drove from Cleveland to Los Angeles in order to make the annual visitation. In a series of letters to the community at the provincial house in Cleveland, Mother Mary Vera described their emotions as the car turned into the driveway, and the three sisters caught their first glimpse of Notre Dame Convent:

> It would be very difficult to describe our emotions when, for the first time, our Cleveland car turned in the driveway of OUR OWN HOME on the WEST COAST. We had left 'home' behind, only to find it again at our destination. And what a HOME it is! In our past visits to California we were, one might say, guests at this affiliation or that affiliation. This time our convent home was the central point from which our activities radiated.[69]

Regarding the convent itself, Mother Mary Vera wrote:

> How we wish you could see our convent home in Los Angeles. God has been good to us....There are many future possibilities here. Their chapel is devotional and beautiful despite its poverty....The beginnings are laborious and blessed with many crosses, but we can all feel God's visible blessings and approval and we know, you will help us thank Him.[70]

Despite the house's imposing exterior, the sisters' lifestyle reflected a true simplicity.

> The interior of the convent contains only bare necessities and gives evidence of poverty. For example, the rug and runner in the entrance lobby is threadbare in many

---

69   This paragraph, written by Mother Mary Vera Niess, S.N.D. was to be included in a letter from the Sisters in the Cleveland Provincial House, Christmas 1945. ASNDC.
70   Mother Mary Vera [Niess], S.N.D., Letter to Sister M. Agnes [Boche] et al. October 30, 1945. ASNDC.

places. The convent does not have one piece of parlor furniture. The pews in the chapel are borrowed. They have no washing machine. All of the laundry is done either by hand or sent to Huntington Park. They have no study hall desks for the sisters who will teach here. Although the convent building itself is magnificent, poverty, we can assure you, reigns within.[71]

"Little" Notre Dame

Notre Dame Students, 1946

Plans for an elementary school on the Overland site had been underway since the previous spring and classes were scheduled

---

71   The Three Travelers [Sister Mary Jeanita Fitz, S.N.D.], Letter to Sister Mary Agnes [Boche] et al. Undated. ASNDC.

to begin on February 1, 1946. However, problems concerning rezoning the site for educational purposes arose. As a result, construction did not actually start until September 1945. Repeated rain delayed the work even further. Although the contractor, Mr. Pierson, had promised to have two rooms ready for use in time for the beginning of classes, now scheduled for April 1, by the end of March the tile floor had not been laid. Once again it rained. Sister Mary William Gara, the first principal, wrote to Mother Mary Vera:

> There wasn't the slightest chance of taking thirty-three little ones into a building– the whole grounds around it was flooded with water – the building itself was damp and cold – no flooring – and still NOTRE DAME would open on April 1. We simply had to open. We simply couldn't go into that building. There was only one thing to do and that was to open school in the Convent. We began to work, clearing the room above the Chapel and moving Sister Mary Celestine out of her workshop. The men came to assemble the desks. We gave up waiting for the rain to stop. They [the men] carried the desks through the rain into the house. Sunday was spent in making the improvised classroom look attractive. We borrowed portable blackboards from St. Francis, and managed quite well with everything else. Sunday night all was in readiness – Grade one in the sewing room, and grades two and three in the large room.[72]

By the following Monday, April 8, 1946, the promised two classrooms were ready, so Sister Mary William, Sister Mary Gladys and their students moved into the new building. In the fall, five more sisters joined the Academy faculty. On September 10, 1946, Notre Dame Academy, the first community-owned school on the west coast, began a full year of classes.

---

72   Sister Mary William [Gara], S.N.D., Letter to Mother Mary Vera [Niess], April 2, 1946. ASNDC.

Approximately three weeks later, on Sunday, September 29, 1946, Auxiliary Bishop-Elect Timothy Manning[73] presided at the dedication of the school. No sooner had the sisters and their guests assembled on the west lawn for the opening prayers, than drops of rain began to fall. By the time the procession had circled the school and returned to the lawn, the rain had stopped. The Bishop ended his remarks at the conclusion of the ceremony with words that were both a hope and a prophecy.

> You know, the dedication of a new school is like the coming of a man-child in the family and the christening of that child. Heaven itself has seen fit to participate in that christening by sending the little shower of rain, just enough to sprinkle the new building. And from the day of its christening it will begin to bear fruit. Today the new school is christened, bears the name of Notre Dame, and is placed under the patronage of Our Blessed Mother. No project under her patronage can fail, – that which is dedicated to Mary must succeed.[74]

The Annex

Notre Dame Academy Elementary School had opened in September 1946 with grades one through six. With the addition of the seventh grade the following autumn, the building had reached capacity. Construction, therefore, was begun on a two-story annex which would provide two classrooms on the first floor for the junior high students and additional living space for the sisters on the second. When the first eighth graders registered in September 1948, however, the annex was not finished. As a result, the eighth grade

---

73   The Most Reverend Timothy Manning was consecrated Auxiliary Bishop of Los Angeles on August 3, 1946. He succeeded Cardinal James Francis McIntyre as Archbishop of Los Angeles on January 21, 1970 and was named a Cardinal Priest on March 5, 1973. Cardinal Timothy Manning died on June 23, 1989.
74   Sisters at Notre Dame Academy, Letter to Mother Mary Vera [Niess] et al., September 29, 1946. ASNDC.

met in the elementary school library while the seventh grade took over the former first grade. This arrangement, however, was only temporary since the sisters planned to use that classroom for a kindergarten which was scheduled to open on October 4th. Fortunately, by the end of September, construction of the annex had reached the point where the two classrooms on the first floor were ready so the junior high students were able to move into their own building.

Notre Dame Academy Girls High School

Notre Dame Academy, 1951

Almost from the beginning of the sisters' apostolate in California, the superiors had envisioned a high school for girls on the west coast. In 1935, Mother Mary Evarista had written to Bishop Cantwell about the possibility of such a school in

Huntington Park.[75] Six years later, 1941, Archbishop Cantwell had given the sisters permission to purchase property in North Hollywood for that purpose. Due to building restrictions and financial difficulties, however, plans had never materialized.[76] In fact, Mother Mary Vera had purchased the property on Overland Avenue in 1944 only after making certain that the four and one half acres would be adequate for a high school as well as an elementary school. However, by 1947-1948, a restructuring of the lines of financial responsibility between the community in Cleveland and the convents on the west coast seemed to mean that construction of a high school would not take place in the foreseeable future.

At that time, the sisters assigned to California were part of the Province of Christ the King. As such, they were members of the Corporation of the Sisters of Notre Dame of Cleveland. As a result any financial obligations that had been incurred by the purchase of the Overland property and the erection of Notre Dame Academy Elementary School were the responsibility of the corporation in Cleveland.

In 1948, however, the houses in California were organized into a corporation distinct from that in Ohio – The Sisters of Notre Dame of Los Angeles. By doing so, the community on the west coast severed its financial ties with the congregation in Cleveland. This meant that the sisters in California were responsible for their own fiscal affairs. In April 1948, Sister Mary Loyole Gabal, as chairman of the newly formed corporation, approached Archbishop Cantwell for permission to borrow $50,000 with which to build the Annex.[77] The need to repay this loan apparently ruled out the possibility of any more construction.

Plans, however, were abruptly changed in the autumn of that year during Mother Mary Agnes Bosche's annual visit

---

75   Mother M. Evarista [Harks], Letter to [Bishop John J. Cantwell], October 7, 1935. AALA. There are also letters in the Archives of the Archdiocese of Los Angeles about possible sites in South Gate (1938) and Arcadia (1941).

76   Joseph T. McGuckin, Chancellor, Letter to Sister Mary Bernardus [sic], January 3, 1941. ASNDC.

77   Bishop Timothy Manning, Memo, April 21, 1948. AALA.

to California.[78] At dinner one evening, Mother Mary Agnes remarked that when the first eighth grade students graduated from the elementary school in June 1949, the girls must be able to enter Notre Dame Academy High School. Sister Mary Madelyn Ryan recalled:

> We all lost our breath. In one chorus we all asked, 'Who is going to do the building?' The answer came very definitely with Mother Mary Agnes' usual smile, 'You people are. Just get busy thinking.' That meant more building – where to get the money. That was up to us. [79]

Since benefit dinners had proved to be successful in Cleveland, the sisters decided to try the same thing in California. Plans were soon underway for a three-day festival climaxed by a ham dinner which would be held on the weekend of May 13, 14 and 15, 1949. One of the sisters reported the outcome to Mother Mary Agnes:

> 'The Ham What Am' carried its power of advertisement so well that we served approximately twelve hundred people…The result of the united efforts of all of us netted a gratifying $12,000—a good beginning for our greater Notre Dame in California.[80]

Even before the festival and dinner were over, plans were underway for the proposed high school. Although the sisters had presented the blueprints to Archbishop James Francis McIntyre, Archbishop Cantwell's successor,[81] in March of that year, finan-

---

78   Sister Mary Agnes (Mary Edna Bosche) entered the novitiate in Cleveland in 1904. Beginning in 1922, she played a major role in the founding of Notre Dame College, Cleveland. She was named superior of Christ the King Province in Cleveland on February 22, 1947 following the election of Mother Mary Vera Neiss as Superior General of the Congregation in December of the previous year. Mother Mary Agnes died on July 21, 1949.
79   Wittenburg, House, 73. ASNDTO
80   Cited in Ibid. 73. A raffle was added the following year. Both activities became annual events.
81   The Most Reverend James Francis McIntyre, Coadjutor Archbishop of New York, was appointed Archbishop of Los Angeles on February 7, 1948. He was created

cial issues delayed the actual start of construction. Nevertheless the sisters were determined to begin classes in September as Mother Mary Agnes wished. As a result the library in the elementary school was transformed into a high school classroom and on September 14, 1949, twenty-eight young women became Notre Dame Academy Girls' High School's first freshman class.

Ground was broken for a permanent building in March 1950 and construction completed the following year. Four years later, 1954-1955, two wings containing a chapel and science lab as well as an auditorium/gym were added.

The spacious new chapel was especially meaningful for the sisters. After more than ten years of temporary chapels the community now had a chapel large enough to accommodate all the sisters assigned to California. Sister Mary William Gara later remarked, "The completion of the chapel at Notre Dame Academy meant a great deal to the sisters in California since…they now had a place where they could all gather for the Eucharistic Sacrifice and for community celebrations." She continued: "How [their] hearts… were filled with joy at the First Holy Mass, when our Eucharistic Lord took up his abode therein." Recalling her own emotions on the day the Chapel of Our Lady, Mother of Grace was dedicated, Sister Mary William concluded: "Thoughts of gratitude to the good God for helping us through this long-desired hope…were secretly offered to the good God. As I stepped forward to light the Sanctuary Lamp, I could hardly control my hand to keep the flame on the wick of the candle."[82]

By the end of the 1950s, Notre Dame Academy had reached its capacity enrollment. In addition to classes in home economic and business, the curriculum included a full four-year college preparatory program. In 1968-1969 the home economics and business tracks were phased out and Notre Dame Academy became a strictly college preparatory high school for girls. The last major change to the high school plant occurred in 1992-1993 when the

Cardinal Priest on January 12, 1953 and died on July 15, 1979.
82   Sister Mary Jessica Karlinger, S.N.D., Personal interview with Sister Mary William Gara, S.N.D., August-September 1987, 3. ASNDTO. Cited hereinafter as Karlinger, Interview, ASNDTO.

front of the auditorium was extended to make room for a two-story addition which included a dance studio and a weight room on the first floor, and an art room, an additional classroom and a second computer lab on the second.

Chapter Four

Rosa Mystica District

Mother Mary Anselm Langenderfer

The possibility that their presence on the west coast might be only temporary was a shadow that darkened the sisters' early years in California. Although Mother Mary Evarista had provided the sisters, the schools in both St. Matthias and St. Lawrence of

Brindisi parishes had been opened primarily through Reverend Mother Mary Cecilia's efforts. Reverend Mother Mary Antonie had shared her predecessor's plans for California. She had personally accepted both St. Rose of Lima School, Maywood (1930), and St. Francis of Assisi School, Los Angeles (1938). It was not until 1941, when Mother Mary Evarista herself agreed to staff St. Helen School in South Gate that the continuance of the sisters' ministry was assured.

At first the houses in California were part of the Province of Christ the King, Cleveland. Sister Mary Bernard, however, dreamed of seeing the California foundations become a province in its own right. In 1946, her dream moved one step closer to reality when, according to the Circular Pertaining to the Acts of the General Chapter, January 1947, the seven houses on the west coast were organized into a district with Sister Mary Loyole Gabal as District Superior.[83] The new district was placed under the patronage of Our Lady, Rosa Mystica.

The title was especially significant. Sister Mary Bernard not only had a strong devotion to the Blessed Mother but also a deep love for California especially for its wide variety of flowers. Sister saw to it that roses were always planted at the convents in which she lived. According to Sister Mary William Gara, when the sisters were asked to choose a name for the newly erected district, Sister Mary Bernard often expressed the hope that the word "rose" would be part of the title. "Imagine her joy and gratitude to God," Sister Mary William said, "that both the ROSE and OUR LADY found their way into the title announced by Reverend Mother Mary Vera."[84]

This arrangement was altered in 1959 when the General Chapter of 1958 organized the houses in California together

---

83   Sister Mary Loyole (Clara Gabal) had come to California in 1944 following a seven-year ministry as Assistant Dean at Notre Dame College (1937-1944). After completing her term as District Superior in 1953, Sister Mary Loyole returned to Notre Dame College to serve, first as local superior and Professor of Philosophy (1953-1955) and then as President (1958-1963). Sister died on July 10, 1981, one week before the celebration of the 60th anniversary of her religious profession.

84   Karlinger, Interview, ASNDTO.

with a number of affiliations in Ohio into the newly erected Julie Billiart Vice-Province. Sister Mary William Gara, who had succeeded Sister Mary Loyole as District Superior in 1953, continued to govern the affiliations on the west coast but now under the jurisdiction of Mother Mary Joseph Geise, former superior of the Province of Immaculate Heart of Mary in Covington, Kentucky.

Rosa Mystica Province

The dissolution of the Julie Billiart Vice-Province in 1961 brought further changes in Rosa Mystica's status. A letter, dated August 22, 1961, announcing Reverend Mother Mary Vera's imminent arrival in California also contained the news that Mother Mary Anselm Langenderfer, former superior of Christ the King Province, Cleveland, would join Reverend Mother Mary Vera and take up her duties as superior in California. Reverend Mother Mary Vera's letter concluded: "Mother, who will then be Sister Mary Anselm, will have the complete powers of a Provincial Superior....The District will, from now on be [a vice-province] under the jurisdiction of the Motherhouse...."[85]

Reverend Mother Mary Vera's arrival on October 23, 1961, however, brought yet another change. Although Reverend Mother's plane landed at Los Angeles International Airport at nearly 11:00 p.m., many of the sisters had gathered in the dining room at Notre Dame Academy to welcome her. As she was discussing the details of Sister Mary Anselm's impending installation, Reverend Mother Mary Vera remarked: "Now in this province..." Noticing the sisters' surprise, she explained, "You know you are a province, don't you?"[86]

Rosa Mystica's new status was officially announced to the sisters of the district on October 28, 1961 when they gathered at

---

85   Letter, August 22, 1961. Cited in <u>Annals</u>, Provincial House Notre Dame Academy, Los Angeles, 1961. ASNDTO.
86   Wittenburg, <u>House</u>, 106. ASNDTO.

Notre Dame Academy for Mother Mary Anselm's installation. Several days later, a postcard announcing the death of a sister in the Congregation posted on the bulletin board in one of the California convents created a good deal of excitement. In print for the first time were the words: "Provincial House, Los Angeles, California."

Mother Mary Anselm was well known to the sisters of the new province since she had previously been Mistress of Novices in Cleveland (1943-1949).[87] Appointed Mother Mary Agnes Bosche's successor in July 1949, Mother Mary Anselm had governed the houses in California as superior of Christ the King Province, Cleveland until 1959 at which time they were incorporated into the Julie Billiart Vice-Province.

Mother Mary Anselm's term as superior of Rosa Mystica Province lasted less than a year. Reverend Mother Mary Vera died unexpectedly on April 14, 1962. The subsequent General Chapter of Election summoned Mother Mary Anselm to Rome the following autumn. The news of Mother Mary Anselm's election as sixth Superior General of the Sisters of Notre Dame on September 12, 1962 was softened shortly thereafter by the announcement that Sister Mary William Gara would succeed her as superior of Rosa Mystica Province.

---

87   Mother Mary Anselm (Hilda Langenderfer) was born in 1901 and entered the Sisters of Notre Dame in Cleveland in 1919. From 1943-1949 Sister served as Mistress of Novices; 1949-1961 as superior of Christ the King Province in Cleveland; 1961-1962, a first superior of Rosa Mystica Province in California, and 1962-1974 as Superior General of the Congregation itself. In 1974, Sister returned to Cleveland where she died on September 27, 1990.

"God's Will-I-Am"

Sr. Mary Loyole Gabal and Sr. Mary William Gara

Sister Mary William (Florence Gara) was born in 1903, the only girl in a family of five boys. After finishing her elementary education at St. Aloysius School, she enrolled in the two-year commercial course at Notre Dame Academy in Cleveland. Although she enjoyed typing and bookkeeping, Florence realized she did not have the subjects necessary to become a teacher.

Consequently, after completing the secretarial program, she re-enrolled at Notre Dame Academy, this time in the four-year academic program. In later years, Sister Mary William remarked that she was grateful to God for this so-called "mistake" since it enabled her to act as her own "secretary" and thus taught her to trust in God's direction in her life. Her personal motto became "God's Will-I-Am."

After graduation from high school, Florence taught elementary school for three years. She entered the novitiate at Cleveland in June 1924. As a second-year novice, Sister Mary William embarked upon her career as a teacher at Gesu School in University Heights. During the next eighteen years, Sister taught various elementary and junior high grades in Ohio, Tennessee and Washington, D.C. In 1945, Sister was transferred to California and named superior and principal of St. Matthias School in Huntington Park. The following year, 1946, she was appointed the first principal of Notre Dame Academy Elementary School in Los Angeles.

Sister Mary William's ministry of leadership began in 1953 when she succeeded Sister Mary Loyole as superior of Rosa Mystica District. At the same time, Sister Mary William was appointed community supervisor for the elementary and secondary schools in California, a responsibility she fulfilled conscientiously for eight and one half years.

Sister Mary William's rich background in education was quickly apparent. Sister initiated and supported innovative approaches to learning on both the elementary and secondary level. During the five years she had spent at the Campus School of the Catholic University of America in Washington, D.C. Sister Mary William had gained a practical knowledge of the principles of Christian Social Living. Consequently, her educational bulletins emphasized the primacy of religion and the necessity of thorough instruction as well as a deep respect for the individual. Much of the sisters' success in the schools at that time can be attributed to Sister Mary William's guidance and direction.

During her twelve years as provincial, Sister Mary William maintained her interest in education. She supported the sisters' professional advancement and fostered a spirit of cooperation between the community and the Archdiocesan officials at the Department of Education. Not only the sisters, but the lay faculty and staff members as well benefited from Sister Mary William's supervisory visits. Her perceptive observations and encouragement conveyed her personal interest and deep appreciation of their work.

Sister Mary William's position as community supervisor of schools was especially advantageous to her both as District Superior and later as Provincial Superior of Rosa Mystica. Sister Mary William herself stated:

> I discovered that I would get to know the sisters by visiting each of the affiliations. In almost every case, the conversation dealt with how the sister was getting along in school...her successes and problems, her feeling of failure. This was actually the best way since it led to a more personal exchange when [I was] assigned as provincial.[88]

Sister Mary William's term as provincial (1962-1974) coincided with the period of self-study, adaptation and change in religious life immediately following Vatican Council II. Sister approached the process of change with an outward calm and deep trust in the providence of God. The manner in which she implemented the Declarations of the Special General Chapter of 1968 revealed not only her own broadmindedness and understanding of human nature, but her sensitivity to California's particular challenges as well.

Through her gift of writing and synthesizing spiritual material, Sister Mary William continuously offered the sisters insights for interior growth. Her letters and instructions not only reveal her deep concern for the spiritual, intellectual and physical

---

88   Karlinger, "Interview," 7. ASNDTO.

well-being of the sisters but also afford an insight into Sister's own interior life and her ability to share the best of what she read and heard.

Beginning a Novitiate

In her letter accepting Bishop Cantwell's invitation to come to California, Reverend Mother Mary Cecilia had expressed the hope that "the bright hope for vocations" which the Bishop had mentioned would soon be realized. The first young woman from California to enter the novitiate in Cleveland was Mary Esparza, a former student from St. Lawrence of Brindisi School.[89] During the ensuing years, five more women followed Mary into the novitiate in Cleveland: Sister Mary Louise Wanamaker (1929), Sister Mary Lenore Bott (1930), Sister Mary Janette Dresman (1932), Sister Mary Joel Upmeier (1934) and Sister Doris Marie McDonald, formerly Sister Mary Leogene (1941).

However, the distance from Los Angeles to Cleveland made entering the community difficult for others. Therefore, in addition to the news that the houses in California were now a district, Reverend Mother Mary Vera's Easter letter[90] had also contained permission to open a postulancy in California as soon as it was feasible.

Establishing a second postulancy and ultimately a novitiate in the same province required a special Apostolic Indult from the Holy See. Therefore, in a letter to Cardinal James Francis McIntyre, dated October 18, 1948, Mother Mary Agnes outlined the reasons why, in addition to the distance between California and Ohio, such an action was justified: namely, the change in climate which some candidates found harmful and the opportunity for parents to attend their daughter's Investment and Profession ceremonies which was at present denied to those who could not

---

89   Mary Esparza (Sister Mary Benigna) was professed on January 2, 1930 and returned to Southern California in 1937. She died on August 22, 1995 in the 65th year of her religious profession.

90   This letter served as an introduction to Acts of the 1947 General Chapter

afford the trip to Cleveland. Mother Mary Agnes also pointed out that the superiors intended to eventually organize the houses in California as a separate province. Lastly, the establishment of a second novitiate on the west coast would be an important means of fostering religious vocations in the Archdiocese of Los Angeles.[91]

Once permission to open a postulancy had been received, plans moved ahead rapidly. In a letter addressed to Mother Mary Agnes and Sister Mary Loyole, dated July 2, 1947, Reverend Mother Mary Vera outlined plans for a future novitiate and named Sister Mary Loyole Mistress of Postulants. [92]

"Sister Peggy"

The Feast of the Holy Rosary, October 7, 1948, patronal feast of the newly erected Rosa Mystica District, was chosen as the first entrance day. That afternoon, Margaret Mary "Peggy" Ballard (Sister Mary Rose Anthony) from St. Francis of Assisi Parish received her cape from Mother Mary Agnes in a simple ceremony at Notre Dame Convent. Since the District House did not yet have separate quarters for postulants, Peggy shared a bedroom and ate and studied with the professed sisters. The arrival of a second postulant, Antonia Napolitano (Sister Mary Francis John), who had been an aspirant in Cleveland for the previous three years, on December 8, 1948, however, necessitated the arrangement of separate facilities for the postulants. Although Peggy and Tony still shared the large bedroom on the second floor of the convent with two professed sisters, the two smaller rooms next to the kitchen in what had once been the Bains' servants' quarters became the postulants' study hall and dining room.

---

91   Mother Mary Agnes, S.N.D., Letter to The Most Reverend James Francis McIntyre, D.D., October 18, 1948. AALA.
92   [Mother Mary] Mary Vera. Letter to Mother Mary Agnes and Sister Mary Loyole, July 2, 1947. ASNDC.

Investment/Profession

Investment Notre Dame Convent 1964

The General Chapter of 1946 had given permission to open only the postulancy in California.[93] Although the postulants would be invested with the religious habit in California, they were to make their novitiate in Cleveland. Therefore, as summer approached, Peggy and Tony's thoughts turned to their investment and their impending trip to Ohio to begin their novitiate. However, Reverend Mother Mary Vera decided that the newly invested novices should remain in California. On August 23, 1949, Peggy, now known as Sister Mary Rose Anthony, and Tony, Sister Mary Francis John, received the habit of the Sisters of Notre Dame. With their reception, the novitiate in California was formally inaugurated with Sister Mary Madelyn Ryan as Mistress of Novices.

During the next two years, the California novitiate grew slowly but steadily. In June of the following year, 1950, the two first-year novices were joined by two postulants, Rosemary Goodman (Sister Mary Serra) and Joann Schlarbaum (Sister Mary Joann,

---

93   Ibid.

formerly Sister Mary John Thomas), former aspirants from California who had entered in Cleveland. A third postulant, Olga Kasunic (Sister Mary Rita Ann) had entered in California the previous September.

On Thursday, August 23, 1951, Sister Mary Rose Anthony and Sister Mary Francis John made their first Profession of Vows. The occasion marked another milestone in the history of the Sisters of Notre Dame in California since it was the first time such a ceremony had taken place on the west coast. Previously, postulants from California had celebrated their first Profession in Cleveland. It also meant the opening of a juniorate under the guidance of Sister Mary Pauletta Sibbing as Mistress of Juniors.[94]

By 1953, however, the novitiate had outgrown its quarters in the convent. Sister Mary Loyole was eager to completely separate the novices and postulants from the professed sisters. However, she was unable to find suitable property on which to erect a permanent building. Therefore, she decided to move the novitiate to the second floor of the elementary school's junior high building, known as the Annex. The south end of the building became the novices and postulants' dormitories, while the large center room served as a combination study hall/dining room. "A crack in the floor divided the study hall from the refectory," Sister Marilynn Palenchar (formerly Sister Mary Michael Claire) recalled. "On one side you could talk and on the other side you couldn't. The scullery was another section of the refectory floor. Life became very cozy indeed."[95]

Rancho La Pilarica

Sister Mary Loyole's successor, Sister Mary William, and her assistant, Sister Mary Pauletta, continued to search for property

---

94 Sister Mary Pauletta (Marie Sibbing) was born on May 18, 1905 and professed as a Sister of Notre Dame on August 16, 1929. In addition to serving as Mistress of the Junior Professed (1951-1975), Sister Mary Pauletta was also Assistant Provincial (1961-1975) and District/Provincial Treasurer (1953-1981). Sister died on May 25, 1991.
95 Cited in Wittenburg, House, 81. ASNDTO.

on which to erect a permanent novitiate building, but each site was rejected for one reason or another. Finally, the sisters decided to purchase the 72-acre estate of Mr. and Mrs. Joseph Breen in Hidden Valley, a residential enclave in Thousand Oaks, north of Los Angeles.

During her visit to California in the summer of 1957, Reverend Mother Mary Vera also toured the property. Reverend Mother was especially pleased with the Breens' former residence which stood on a small hill approximately 1,870 feet above the floor of the valley. West of the house was a swimming pool and, beyond that, a comparatively level area on which a permanent novitiate building could eventually be built. The rest of property was heavily wooded and would provide the seclusion the superiors wanted. Best of all was the name of the estate – "Rancho La Pilarica".[96] The sisters opened negotiations for the purchase of property almost immediately, and on August 30, 1957, the thirty-third anniversary of the sisters' arrival in California, the acreage was placed in escrow. Reverend Mother Mary Vera herself chose Saturday, October 12, 1957, the Feast of Our Lady of the Pillar, as the day for the blessing of the house and the celebration of the first Mass.

As a special surprise, Reverend Mother Mary Vera asked Sister Mary Antonin Claes in Spain to purchase an authentic statue of Our Lady of the Pillar. The statue was sent to Sister Mary Verona Tepe at the Motherhouse in Rome who took it to Castel Gandolfo where it was blessed by Pope Pius XII. Sister Mary Hildegara Heinz then brought the statue to Rancho La Pilarica in the autumn of 1957 where it was solemnly enthroned during a special Holy Hour on December 8, the Feast of the Immaculate Conception.

Almost immediately after the purchase of the Breen estate, architects began drawing blueprints for a permanent building. Although ground was broken on Sunday November 2, 1958, work

---

96   Mr. Breen explained that on his trips to Europe he had been impressed by the tremendous devotion the people of Spain had shown to the Blessed Virgin under the title, "Our Lady of the Pillar." As a result, he had decided to name his estate in her honor, Rancho La Pilarica. Ibid.

did not begin until May of the following year, 1959. Construction was completed in the spring of 1961. On Thursday morning, June 1, following the celebration of the first Mass, Sister Mary William lit the sanctuary lamp in the novitiate chapel.

Pilarica College

Hidden Valley Novitiate

Study Hall

*Kristin Battles PND, Sr. Antoinette Marie Moon NND, and
Sr. Mary Bernadette Pendola NND at Study Hall*

Transferring the novitiate to Hidden Valley created difficulties relevant to the education of the novices and postulants. From the onset of the sisters' ministry in California, first Sister Mary Bernard, then Sister Mary Loyole and finally Sister Mary William had made certain that the sisters received both the degrees and credentials necessary to carry out their professional responsibilities. When they lived at the District House the novices and postulants took classes at Mt. St. Mary's College, approximately a thirty-minute drive from Notre Dame. The transfer of the novitiate to Hidden Valley, however, meant that the novices and postulants now faced at least an hour's drive to and from Mount St. Mary's, a fact which seriously curtailed the number and type of courses in which the they could enroll.

Reverend Mother Mary Vera, however, had foreseen this problem. In addition to sanctioning the purchase of the Breen estate, she had authorized the establishment of a two-year liberal arts college affiliated with the Catholic University of American in Washington, D.C. at Rancho La Pilarica.[97]

Early in December 1957, Sister Mary William opened negotiations with Catholic University. In October 1958 Pilarica College was granted formal affiliation subject to examination by the authorities after two years.[98] Sister Mary Denis Rinehart, former Dean of Notre Dame College in Cleveland, was named Dean. The first convocation was held on Sunday, September 20, 1959. Regular classes began the next day.

In the beginning the faculty was small. In addition to Sister Mary Denis, who taught English Composition, Sister Mary Ellen Schnee (formerly Sister Mary St. Ellen) and Sister Mary Joel Upmeier traveled from Notre Dame Academy in Los Angeles twice a week for classes in French and history. Once a week, a priest from St. John's Seminary in Camarillo celebrated Mass in the novitiate chapel and then taught a class in Theology or Scripture to the novices and postulants. In addition, Father

---

97   The college was originally called Notre Dame Community Junior College. At that time, however, it was commonly believed that students enrolled in a junior college were not financially and scholastically able to attend a four-year college. Since the college was not a terminus institution but a two-year preparation, the name was changed to Pilarica College in May 1961.

98   Letter from Mother Mary William, S.N.D., May 13, 1969. ASNDTO.

Carroll O'Sullivan, from Santa Clara High School, Oxnard, lectured twice a week in philosophy.

During the next two years, the curriculum was expanded to include classes in physical geography, math, Latin, French and literature. As long as the sisters lived in the ranch house, teaching conditions were somewhat makeshift; but once the sisters moved into the permanent novitiate building the students had the luxury of formal classrooms with stationary chalk boards and authentic lecture chairs. On Saturday, June 10, 1961, four second-year novices and three junior professed sisters were the first students to receive an Associate of Arts Degree from Pilarica College.

In the spring of 1969, Catholic University announced it was discontinuing its Program of Affiliation. Sister Mary Ralph Fahey, as Dean, immediately petitioned the administration of Mount St, Mary's College to permit Pilarica College to become an extension. The request was granted and Pilarica College became the "Pilarica Extension Campus of Mount St. Mary's College."[99]

---

99   Letter from Mother Mary William, S.N.D., May 13, 1969. ASNDTO.

The Preps

Pilarica

Seven Enter the Novitiate, 1960

The transfer of the novitiate to Hidden Valley in 1957 came none too soon for the young women in the aspirant school. Since its opening in 1949, the "preps," as they were known, had occupied rooms in every building on the Notre Dame Academy campus – the convent as well as both the elementary and high school. By 1957, however, the aspirants had outgrown their quarters so their move into the Annex, the novitiate's former residence, in the fall of 1957, was a welcome one.

The Villa, as the second floor of the Annex was known, was "Prepville" for the next thirteen years. In 1970, the change in the Church's attitude toward early vocations following Vatican Council II coupled with the sisters' own need for more living space, ultimately brought about the closure of the aspirant school. By that time, twenty-one sisters could boast of beginning their religious life in Notre Dame with A.N.D. after their name.

"In obedience, we go to Thousand Oaks."

From 1947 to 1965, Notre Dame Academy had served as the administrative headquarters for the Sisters of Notre Dame in California– first as the District House (1947-1961), then as the Provincial House (1961-1965). In as much as the novitiate was now in Thousand Oaks, both Reverend Mother Mary Vera and her successor, Reverend Mother Mary Anselm, wanted the provincial administration located on the same site. Preliminary plans for the transfer had been underway for several months, but the news became official on July 12, 1965 when Mother Mary William prefaced the 1965-1966 appointments with the announcement: "In obedience, we go to Thousand Oaks." [100]

Several weeks of packing, labeling and coding under the direction of Sister Mary Pauletta culminated on August 25, 1965 when the members of the provincial administration moved into the ranch house at Rancho La Pilarica, By the time Mother Mary William concluded her term of office in 1974, it was obvious that

---

100   Wittenburg, House, 107. ASNDTO.

housing the administration of Rosa Mystica Province at Rancho La Pilarica could only be temporary. Therefore, it would be up to Sister Mary William's successor, Sister Mary Francelia Klingshirn, to build a permanent provincial house.

Novices enjoying recreation time at Rancho La Pilarica

Sr. Mary Joyanne Sullivan, and Sr. Dwina Marie Towle

Sr. Mary Amy Hauck at Dodger Stadium

Chapter Five

Expansion

Province Portrait 1963

The following years were ones of expansion and celebration. During the next thirty-five years (1945-1980) the community's apostolate on the west coast reached its greatest extent. At the conclusion of World War II, Southern California's population exploded as former service men and employees in the aircraft and space technology industries chose to remain in the area. In 1940 Los Angeles County registered a population of 504,131 individuals. By 1960, the county's population had risen to 2,208,492,[101] an increase of slightly more than 400 %.

The Catholic population mushroomed as well. By 1975, the number of Catholics in the Archdiocese of Los Angeles rose from 520,000 in 1945 to 2,208,989. One hundred fifteen new parishes

---

101   Gerhard F. Thornton, (ed.), The Los Angeles Almanac 2001 Montebello, California: Given Place Publishing Company, 2001, 413.

had been erected as well as 161 elementary and 33 new high schools built.[102] Responsive to the needs of the Church, the sisters accepted eleven of these elementary schools as well as four high schools during these years

The sisters' purchase of the Overland Avenue property and the subsequent opening of Notre Dame Academy Elementary School introduced the community to the western part of the Archdiocese. They quickly became involved in a variety of ministries in that area. Beginning in the summer of 1945, the sisters at Notre Dame Academy conducted vacation schools and taught religious education for the public school children in St. Timothy and St. Joan of Arc parishes. In 1947, when the latter parish broke ground for a parochial school, the Sisters of Notre Dame staffed it. The following year, 1948, Mother Mary Agnes agreed to provide sisters for Our Lady of Perpetual Help Parish School in Downey.

The opening of St. Cornelius School, Richmond, in 1949 and St. Paul School, San Pablo, in 1952 brought the sisters' educational ministry into northern California. In September 1958, the community fulfilled Father William O'Shea's dream of an elementary school in his parish when St. Timothy School opened on September 15th. With the community's acceptance of St. David School, also in Richmond, in 1968, the number of schools in the San Francisco/ Oakland area staffed by the Sisters of Notre Dame rose to three.

Since both the novitiate and the provincial house were located in Ventura County, the superiors were eager to expand the community's ministry into that region as well. As a result, the sisters accepted three elementary schools in the Ventura area: Our Lady of the Assumption, Ventura (1958), St. Paschal Baylon, Thousand Oaks (1963) and St. Rose of Lima, Simi Valley (1964).[103]

Lastly, the Sisters of the Immaculate Heart of Mary's decision to withdraw many of their sisters from teaching left many schools in the Archdiocese without a religious faculty. In 1968,

---

102   The Official Catholic Directory, New York: P.J. Kenedy and Sons, Publishers, 1946 and 1976, 130-131, 465-466. The statistics given in the Directory are for the previous year.

103   In the 1980s, the sisters accepted the leadership of two more schools in Ventura County, Sacred Heart in Ventura-Saticoy (1981) and St. Jude the Apostle in Westlake Village (1982).

in response to Cardinal James Francis McIntyre's request for religious women to replace them, the Sisters of Notre Dame took over St. Bernardine of Siena School in Woodland Hills and St. Mary Magdalen School in Camarillo.

Group of Novices and newly professed Sisters, circa 1972

Pius X and St. Bonaventure High Schools

The number of secondary schools in which the sisters taught increased as well. In 1948, the Most Reverend James Francis McIntyre, Auxiliary Bishop of New York, succeeded Archbishop John J. Cantwell to the See of Los Angeles. One of Archbishop McIntyre's priorities was education. Therefore, shortly after his arrival he asked Monsignor Patrick Dignan, the Superintendent of Catholic Schools, to compile a survey showing the educational needs of the Archdiocese, especially in light of the tremendous surge in population following World War II.

The results of the survey were alarming. Although Catholic elementary schools enrolled approximately 48,600 students, another

52,300 were turned away due to lack of room. The same was true of the high schools. Catholic secondary schools could accommodate only 20% of the high school age population. The rest had to go elsewhere. In order to rectify this situation, Archbishop McIntyre launched the Youth Education Fund, what David Halburd described in *Life* magazine as "the most concentrated fund-raising and school building program ever undertaken anywhere."[104]

The Youth Education Fund consisted of four separate campaigns.

The first of these, launched on February 13, 1949, raised a total of $2.8 million. A second campaign, begun in the fall of 1955, was aimed especially at erecting high schools. Two additional campaigns followed in 1958 and 1963.

Among the first high schools erected by the Youth Education Fund was Pius X High School, a large co-educational Archdiocesan institution slated to serve the families in Southeast Los Angeles. In August 1953, the principal, Father Joseph Sharpe, invited Mother Mary Anselm Langenderfer to appoint two sisters to the faculty.[105] In a letter, dated August 23, 1953, Mother responded by naming Sister Mary St. Joseph Feichert, former superior and principal at St. Rose of Lima School, Maywood, and Sister Mary Denis Reinhart, former dean of Notre Dame College, Cleveland.[106] The two sisters remained at Pius X High School until 1958. The Sisters of Notre Dame returned to Pius X in 1968 and remained on the faculty until 1979.

St. Bonaventure High School in Ventura, partially financed with the help of the third Youth Education Fund campaign, was designed to serve the needs of families in Ventura, Ojai, Santa Paula, Fillmore and the surrounding areas. Construction of the first three buildings started on March 2, 1963.[107]

---

104   Cited in Msgr. Francis J. Weber, <u>His Eminence of Los Angeles: James Francis Cardinal McIntyre</u>, Mission Hills, California, St. Francis Historical Society, 1997, Vol. One. 250.

105   Reverend Joseph F. Sharpe, Letter to Mother Mary Anselm, S.N.D., August 3, 1953. ASNDC.

106   [Mother Mary Anselm Langenderfer, S.N.D.], Letter to Rev. Joseph F. Sharpe, August 23, 1953. ASNDC.

107   Initially St. Bonaventure High School accommodated 450 students. Later expansion would bring the total capacity to 600.

Classes officially began the following September. Since the new high school was on the same property as Our Lady of the Assumption Elementary School, Mother Mary William agreed to provide sisters for the first faculty. Sister Mary St. Lawrence Begin was appointed principal.

Two years later, in 1965, Father Joseph Pekarcik, an arch-diocesan priest, was named Director in place of Sister Mary St. Lawrence. The following autumn, Father Thomas Meskill suc-ceeded Father Pekarcik. Sister Marilynn Palenchar, (formerly Sister Mary Michael Claire), became Dean of Girls and two Irish Franciscan Brothers joined the faculty.

The growth of the community's ministry in secondary educa-tion was not confined to these two new archdiocesan high schools. In 1960, the community opened St. Matthias High School thereby fulfilling the sisters' long-held dream of a four-year high school for girls in Huntington Park. Four years later, 1964, the commu-nity broke ground for La Reina High School in Thousand Oaks, the third community-owned school in Southern California.

St. Matthias High School

From the beginning of the Congregation's apostolate in California, the sisters had hoped to open a four-year high school in Huntington Park. In 1930, a ninth grade had been added to St. Matthias' original eight grades. Twelve years later, in 1942, a tenth grade was opened to accommodate the growing number of families moving into the neighborhood as the result of World War II. The sisters hoped that these two grades would eventually expand into a four-year co-educational high school.

At first, the ninth and tenth grade students used two rooms in the elementary school building. However, by 1950, the grade school's enrollment had reached the point where the teachers needed the classrooms which the high school occupied; conse-quently grades nine and ten were discontinued. The sisters' hope that the community might buy property and build in Huntington Park died when the Archdiocese announced plans to open Pius X High School in order to serve families in southeast Los Angeles.

By 1960, however, Pius X High School had nearly reached its capacity enrollment. At the same time St. Matthias Parish was constructing a new building for the elementary school several blocks south of its present site. Therefore, with the blessing of the Archdiocese, the pastor, Monsignor Patrick Shear, decided to convert the original grade school building into a high school for girls.

St. Matthias High School opened on September 6, 1960 with a freshman class of seventy-six young women. The enrollment grew rapidly. By the following September the number of students had doubled. In May 1962 construction was begun on a new wing which would provide space for administrative offices and a library as well as for science and home economic labs. Coincidently, St. Matthias High School's first graduation took place in June 1964, the year which marked the fortieth anniversary of the sisters' arrival in California.

La Reina High School

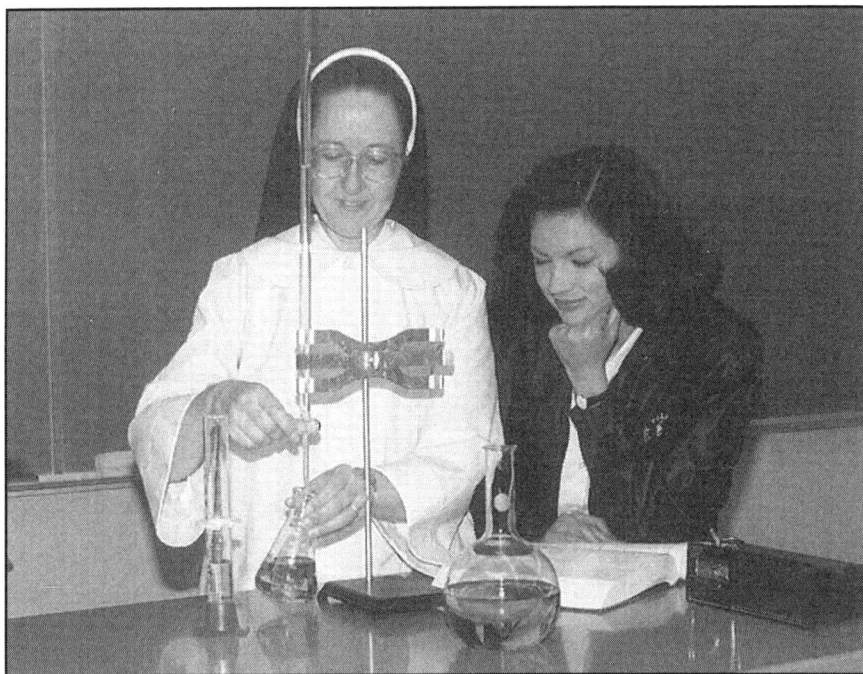

Sr. Mary Joan Schlotfeldt and Dr. Adrienne Bessey M.D.

Plans for La Reina High School had actually been underway since 1959, five years before its official opening in September 1964. At the request of Reverend Mother Mary Vera, Mother Mary William had searched for property in the San Fernando and Conejo Valleys as well as in San Bernardino and Orange counties in hopes of finding a site suitable for a second community high school and possibly a new provincial house. Finally, on August 2, 1959, Mother Mary William approached Cardinal McIntyre for permission to purchase a twenty-five acre tract of land in the Conejo Valley in Thousand Oaks.[108]

The following autumn Reverend Mother Mary Vera herself visited and approved the site. On October 20, 1959, the community obtained an option from the Janss Corporation, owners of the property, to purchase the twenty-five acre tract for a high school. The purchase was completed on October 24, 1963.

On February 25, 1964 Mother Mary William unobtrusively broke ground for La Reina High School. Reverend Mother Mary Vera herself had chosen the name from the suggestions which the sisters had submitted thereby acknowledging California's Spanish heritage since it was derived from the original name of the city of Los Angeles, *El Pueblo Nuestra Senora la Reina de los Angeles.* An account in the Annals of the Sisters of Notre Dame, Thousand Oaks, described the simple ceremony:

> Mother Mary William, Sister Mary Pauletta and Sister Mary Cornelia [formerly Sister Mary Cornelius]... went to the site and on the north slope of the hill, scooped out a few handfuls of soil and into the cavity placed several blessed medals. Mother Mary William blessed the land with holy water and all said a few prayers for God's continued guidance and protection on the coming construction.[109]

A week later, bulldozers began leveling a twelve-acre plateau on which the first unit, a ten-classroom building, would be

---

108   Sister Mary William, S.N.D., Letter to The Most Reverend James Francis Cardinal McIntyre, August 2, 1959. AALA.
109   Annals, Rosa Mystica Provincial House, 1964, 7. ASNDTO.

erected. Work progressed rapidly. On September 8, 1964, the sisters welcomed eighteen freshmen.[110]

Almost immediately after the first unit was finished construction was started on the administration building. By April 1965 this unit was ready for occupancy. Work was begun in May 1966 on a multi-purpose building which would contain a chapel, science and homemaking labs and business, art and audio-visual rooms. Before the construction was finished, however, the province's building resources were exhausted. As a result, Mother Mary William told the workmen to leave the chapel unfinished in hopes of completing it at a later date.

Shortly after Mother Mary William had announced her decision; Sister Mary Bernard received an inheritance which the General Council agreed the province could use to complete the chapel. The formal dedication was planned for January 20, 1967. Sister Mary Bernard, however, died on April 16, 1966. Therefore the chapel, dedicated to Mary, Mother of the Church, became a memorial to her in gratitude for her forty-two years of ministry in California.

Golden Jubilee

These years were also ones of celebration. In 1974 the sisters marked the 50th anniversary of their arrival in California. Fifty years before, on August 30, 1924, eleven women had stepped off the train in Los Angeles eager to begin a new ministry on the west coast Now the number stood at 144 sisters serving not only in the Archdiocese of Los Angeles but in the Diocese of Oakland in northern California as well. Since then sixty-two young women had entered the Congregation, fifty-six of whom had been formed in the California novitiate.

The original two elementary schools, St. Matthias and St. Lawrence of Brindisi, had grown to seventeen. In addition, the sisters were teaching in four high schools plus a junior college. Three of these schools – Notre Dame Elementary School, Notre Dame

---

110   La Reina High School originally had a 9-12 configuration. In September 1973, the curriculum was expanded to include a junior high division.

Academy High School, both in Los Angeles, and La Reina High School in Thousand Oaks – were owned by the community itself. Although the majority of the schools were located in predominantly middle class neighborhoods, both St. Lawrence of Brindisi and St. Leo served an economically disadvantaged population.

The year 1974 marked the end of Sister Mary William's twenty years of leadership, first as District Superior and then as provincial of the sisters on the west coast. On July 27, 1974 the sisters celebrated once again when they learned that Sister Mary Francelia Klingshirn had been named to succeed her.

A *"Sister Teacher"*

Sister Mary Francelia (Margaret Klingshirn) was born in 1917 in Elyria, Ohio, Following the death of her mother when she was eight years old, Margaret and her siblings were raised by their maternal grandmother who, Sister later wrote, taught us "honesty, hard work, perseverance, and love for God and others."[111] In 1931, Margaret's father remarried, thus adding four and eventually three more half-brothers and sisters to the family.

Margaret first encountered the Sisters of Notre Dame as an elementary school student. She completed her secondary education in public institutions however, since no Catholic high schools were available in the area. From the age of eight, Margaret had wanted to become a "Sister teacher" and to work with little children. Therefore, at the age of seventeen, she entered the Sisters of Notre Dame and completed her senior year as a postulant at Notre Dame Academy in Cleveland.

Following her profession in 1938, Sister Mary Francelia ministered first as a teacher, then as principal in various elementary schools in Ohio and Washington, D.C. Sister came to California in 1962 and served as teacher, superior and principal first at St. Matthias Elementary School (1962-1965) and then at Our Lady of the Assumption School, Ventura. In 1971, Sister Mary Francelia was named School Supervisor for the Notre Dame schools in California.

---

111   Account by Sister Mary Francelia Klingshirn, S.N.D., n.d. ASNDTO.

This appointment, which she held for three years, gave Sister the opportunity to share her love of education and expertise in the training and supervision of teachers with the sisters and lay teachers of the California province. Recalling her response to this ministry, Sister said: "Although I had 'lost my school, my children' I soon found that the opportunities to share my love for teaching had multiplied, and my days were filled with challenges and joys of seeing the enthusiasm and willingness to learn in both teachers and children."[112]

On December 14, 1974, Sister Mary Francelia was installed as superior of Rosa Mystica Province. Among the challenges facing Sister as she began her term was finalizing the plans for a new provincial house in Thousand Oaks, California.

Notre Dame Center

Sr. Mary Francelia Klingshirn breaking ground at the new Notre Dame Center while Sr. Mary Joann Schlarbaum, and Sr. Mary Pauletta Sibbing look on.

112   Ibid.

Notre Dame Center

Accounts in the <u>Annals</u> of the Provincial House as well as letters in the archives of the Archdiocese of Los Angeles indicate
that the superiors had considered building a provincial house
in the Thousand Oaks area as early as 1959. In 1961, the sisters obtained a second option from the Janss Corporation for
an additional twenty-five acres north of land adjacent to the La
Reina High School site. The title cleared escrow on January 24,
1963 and the entire fifty-acre site became the property of the
Sisters of Notre Dame.

Originally the sisters hoped to build on the low hill located
near the western boundary of the property. However, the cost of
leveling the hill and then building was financially prohibitive;
therefore, the architects drew up plans for a two-story building
for the level section north of the hill and facing Hendrix Avenue.
On Monday, August 15, 1977, Reverend Colm O'Ryan, Associate
Pastor at St. Paschal Baylon Parish, blessed the site. Then in the
presence of approximately 120 sisters and their guests, Sister

Mary Francelia broke ground for the new building by turning the first shovel of dirt.

The plans for the construction of Notre Dame Center indicated that the work would take place in three phases. The first phase consisted of building three modules: the kitchen/dining/laundry/infirmary unit, administration/reception unit, and finally the unit containing bedrooms for the sisters. At the same time, the workers would complete the landscaping and walkways as well as pour the foundation for the fourth module which would contain classrooms and a library, quarters for the novices and postulants and additional bedrooms for the sisters. The interior of this last unit would remain unfurnished until a later date. The final phase, construction of the chapel, would take place in the future. Within three months of the ground breaking construction of Phase One was underway.

Obviously, it was impossible for the community to undertake the construction of Notre Dame Center, and still maintain the property in Hidden Valley. Moreover, the cost of fire insurance due to the threat of forest fires had become prohibitive. Furthermore, Sister Mary Francelia recalled: "It had become increasingly difficult to provide for our elderly sisters during fire evacuations and in health care emergencies."[113] Therefore, beginning in 1976, the sisters initiated the steps necessary to sell what everyone fondly called "the ranch." On January 23, 1979, title to Rancho La Pilarica passed to David Murdock, chairman of the Murdock Development Company of Los Angeles, and owner of Ventura Farms, a ranch also located in Hidden Valley.

In the meantime, the construction of the first three units of Notre Dame Center was nearly finished. Almost the entire month of March 1979 was taken up with moving furniture and the like into the new building. Finally on Friday, March 30th Sister Mary Francelia and five other members of the provincial community moved into the Center. "There were no elevators, heat or hot water," Sister Mary Francelia later wrote, "but the sisters at St. Paschal Baylon and La Reina convents took care of our needs for

---

113   Sister Mary Francelia Klingshirn, S.N.D., "Transfer of Provincial House," n.d. ASNDTO. .

meals and showers."[114] By May 20th the other members of the provincial house community, including the novices and postulants,
who had been living at Notre Dame Academy and other convents
in Ventura County, had joined them as well.

Construction to complete the fourth wing unit which contained classrooms and a library together with rooms for the novitiate as well as additional bedrooms for the sisters began almost
immediately. At the same time planning for the fifth and final
module which contained the chapel was well underway. Actual
construction began in March, 1980, and was finished by the following autumn.

Sunday, November 21 was the day chosen for the dedication of Queen of the Rosary Chapel. The chapel itself contained
three significant features. The sanctuary light holder, the base of
the tabernacle and two ornate candle holders had been crafted
from the sterling silver crucifixes which the sisters had worn until
they were replaced by the smaller pewter cross four years earlier.
The ambo, the pedestal for the tabernacle as well as the altar
itself contained original mosaics designed by Sister Mary St. Ann
Paskert.[115] Lastly, in to these mosaics, Sister Mary Francelia had
cemented stones which she had personally collected from the
crypt of St. Peter's Basilica, from the Catacombs in Rome, from
St. Julie's birthplace in Cuvilly, from the first convent in Coesfeld,
from the Provincial Motherhouse in Mulhausen and from the
Motherhouse in Rome.

Two weeks later the sisters initiated a series of open houses
to celebrate the completion of Notre Dame Center. On Sunday
December 7, the eve of the feast of the Immaculate Conception,
Cardinal Timothy Manning celebrated Mass and blessed the
building. Following this, the sisters hosted an open house for
the priests and sisters of the archdiocese. On the next weekend, December 13 and 14, the sisters' friends and relatives were
invited to tour Notre Dame Center.

---

114   Ibid.
115   Sister Mary St. Ann Paskert also created the mosaic on the front of the
planter in the foyer. She also helped each sister in the province create a personal tile
for the fireplace in the community room.

Notre Dame Center meant many things to many people. To the sisters of the provincial administration it meant finally having adequate space for offices and archives after nearly fourteen years of working in rather cramped quarters in the former "ranch house." For the sisters on the health care staff it meant a fully equipped infirmary.

In the 1920s California was seen as a place to go for improving one's health. That was Mother Mary Cecilia's mind when she accepted St. Matthias and St. Lawrence of Brindisi schools. Weak and ailing sisters were frequently sent to the west coast. As soon as their health became debilitating, however, they returned to the infirmary in Cleveland. This pattern continued up until the mid 1960s. Then sisters who became terminally ill or needed post-operative care were sent to Notre Dame Academy. Since the convent was formerly a private residence, the rooms designated as the infirmary were not as conveniently arranged as one might have wished. Now the sister-nurses could care for the ill and elderly members of the province in a more professional environment.

To Sister Mary Francelia it meant the end of the many "challenges, changes in plans, decisions and new expenses." There was also a deep sense of gratitude:

> for Sister Mary Pauletta's foresight and financial acumen, for Sister Mary Cornelia's experience and ability to read blueprints, for the artistic skill of Al Czubiac our architect, and for the support of Sister Mary Joann and the sisters of the province. Notre Dame Center had the character, the versatility and the beauty that we had all hoped for.[116]

---

116   Ibid.

Challenges

The stories associated with the opening of the schools and convents in both Northern and Southern California reflect a wide variety of experiences. When the sisters arrived at Our Lady of Perpetual Help Parish in Downey in August, there was no school. The previous year, 1947, the parish had purchased a three and one and a half acre estate on Downey Avenue complete with swimming pool, tennis courts and rumpus house. The cost of renovating the residence for the sisters' use, however, had exceeded the parish's budget, so the pastor, Father Patrick Carey, had decided to postpone construction of the school itself until January of the following year.

What is more, the three places which were to serve as temporary classrooms – the hall next to the church, the rumpus house across from the swimming pool and the large garage – were not ready for use. Consequently the sisters spent the next two weeks removing cobwebs, scrubbing and polishing floors, arranging classroom equipment and turning sheets of cardboard into bulletin boards and boxes and cartons into bookcases so that classes could begin on September 13, 1948 as planned.

More often, the <u>Annals</u> of the various convents note, the school building was still under construction when the first sisters arrived. Although St. Helen Parish had broken ground for the school in 1941, war time restrictions had repeatedly delayed its construction. Consequently, the building would not be ready for occupancy until December. Rather than postpone the opening of school, the sisters decided to begin classes on September 29, 1941, as scheduled, although in a variety of settings.

The first grade met on the cement driveway next to the convent while the second and third grades met in the church. When the primary session was dismissed at 10:00 a.m., fourth and fifth graders assembled in the church while the sixth grade gathered around card tables set up on the convent driveway. After lunch, the eighth grade took over the church while the seventh grade occupied tables, pews and chairs in a shady part of the convent yard.[117]

St. Helen Church itself was quite small: sixteen pews stretched across the width of the church separated only by a narrow aisle.[118] Sister Mary Joann Schlarbaum, (formerly Sister Mary John Thomas) who was in the fourth grade at the time, remembered what it was like to have classes in church.

> The session lasted only two hours. We sat on the kneelers and wrote on the pews. In those days, we bought all our books, so every day we would carry everything we needed for class back and forth from home since there was no place to store anything in the church. There was a portable blackboard which both classes took turns using. The presence of another grade in the same room wasn't really disturbing since we were very much aware of the fact that we were in church. However, whenever it rained, we had to share the church with a third class. Then things did get a little crowded.[119]

At St. Joan of Arc as well, the building was only partially finished when the sisters saw the school for the first time in late August 1947. "We tried in vain to organize classrooms, equipment, supplies, procedures," Sister Mary Bernard wrote:

> There were no doors, locks, blackboards or cloakrooms, and the floors were not completed. All we could see was lumber, bags of plaster, tools, and everything that belonged to the workingman's equipment. We wondered if all the debris would disappear within a week.[120]

When the sisters returned on registration day, September 5, an amazing transformation had taken place: floors had been

---

117   Letter, November 1941. ASNDC.
118   Ibid.
119   Wittenburg, House, 36. ASNDTO.
120   Ibid. 59.

tiled, chalkboards installed, doors hung and classrooms arranged. Moreover, not a workman was in sight. But no sooner had the last child left the building than the plumbers, plasterers, painters, electricians, carpenters and inspectors reappeared and continued to make their presence felt for the next two months.

Sisters who taught in a high school frequently faced a similar situation. Recalling the first days at St. Bonaventure High School in Ventura, Sister Mary Mercedes Louy wrote:

> The area was muddy and the building not completed... No windows, in yet – no equipment – and we were to open in a few weeks. The windows had heavy plastic across them...We borrowed tables and chairs from Assumption Hall for desks, etc. and Sister [Mary St, Lawrence] was determined that we would open on schedule.[121]

The sisters frequently faced a similar situation in regards to the convent. Sometimes their first home was a renovated building. At St. Lawrence of Brindisi, it was a farmhouse; at St. Francis of Assisi, a "dilapidated old parish hall;"[122] at St. Helen, the former rectory. At St. Timothy, St. Bernardine of Siena, St. Paschal Baylon, and St. Rose of Lima in Simi, the parish purchased a private home which, with minor alternations, became the convent.

At other times, although the building itself was new, it was not finished when the sisters arrived. When this happened, the sisters assigned to the school usually commuted from another affiliation as in the case of Our Lady of the Assumption, and St. Paschal Baylon schools. At St. Paul in San Pablo, the sisters decided to move in anyway in order to hurry the workmen along. Sister Mary José Koenig recalled:

> Father hurried to get desks for us so we'd have something to sit on for study. The beds were in. We had no

---

121   Ibid. 114.
122   Letter, September 1938. ASNDC.

refectory table so we borrowed a table and chairs from the hall. We had a chapel but no Blessed Sacrament."[123]

At St. Timothy, the sisters offered to live in the school temporarily until the convent was finished. The faculty room served as the refectory, scullery, workroom, and storeroom while an empty classroom on the second floor became a dormitory. "The mattresses had already arrived for the beds for the convent," Sister Mary Lois Remark remembered.

> The large cardboard boxes in which they [the mattresses] were stored were taken apart and laid on the floor for protection. Four mattresses were carefully laid on top of the cardboard and beds were made with the kind assistance of the Sisters at Notre Dame Academy who gave us sheets and pillow cases, and the blankets were furnished by Father O'Shea [the pastor]...With a few borrowed screens for privacy [we] planned a schedule. Two would use the girls' restroom, one the Health Clinic and the other the faculty room. Each one took turns during the night to take care of the strange noises – mosquitoes, spiders, cockroaches, etc.[124]

Even when the sisters arrived to find the school and convent ready for occupancy, many times things in the way of school supplies and household items were missing. Frequently the sisters' recollections of their pioneering days included such comments as "We managed to borrow some of the textbooks we needed from the other California houses." "Bulletin boards were missing but large pieces of cardboard worked just as well." "We simply did without until we gradually accumulated all we needed."

For the sisters assigned to teach in northern California, separation from the sisters stationed in the south was especially difficult. Sister Mary Bernard had instilled in the sisters a real sense of family and deep appreciation of times when all the sisters

---

123   Wittenburg, House, 77. ASNDTO.
124   Ibid. 94.

could be together. Consequently, the northern sisters' inability to attend the community reunions at Notre Dame Academy at Christmas and Easter was difficult but "The sisters…were magnificent," Sister Mary William Gara, principal and superior at St. Cornelius School in Richmond, later wrote:

> …and in spite of how they might have felt, all [the sisters] helped keep one another's spirit high. That year of 1949 marked the centenary of the community with all its grand celebrations, and also the 25th anniversary of our arrival in California – it was difficult to celebrate with only five sisters, and so far away from the scene of activity. But we made the best of it…by 'pretending'… each sister entered into it [our own celebrations] that we keep our minds off being lonesome…there was a marked enthusiasm in the school, and before long we became so immersed in keeping up with the standards and cooperating with the Mother's Club and finding extreme joy in the children, that we soon forgot that Notre Dame or St. Matthias, or St. Helen's, etc, was not just around the corner.[125]

Yet the narrative in the various <u>Annals</u> and in accounts written to the superiors as well as in Christmas letters to different convents reflect a sense of joy and excitement. Such challenges as these were simply part of the fun of "Beginning!"

---

125   <u>Ibid</u>. 71. ASNDTO.

Sr. Anna Maria Vasquez

Sr. Betty Mae Bienlein

Sr. Carol Marie Papet

Sr. Julie Marie Arriaga

Chapter Six

Toward the New Millennium

The final decades of the twentieth century (1980-2000) coincided with the upheaval in the Church which followed the promulgation of the documents of Vatican Council II. Sister Mary Francelia Klingshirn's term as provincial ended in 1980.[126] On December 20, 1980, Sister Mary Joann Schlarbaum[127] [formerly Sister Mary John Thomas] was installed as fourth superior of Rosa Mystica Province. At that time no one could foresee the changes in religious life that would impact the sisters in Southern California during the next twenty years.

As with most religious communities in the United States, the sisters of the Province of Rosa Mystica experienced a diminishment of both personnel and resources. By the year 2000, the number of sisters on the west coast had decreased to seventy-six and the number of schools to eleven. On both the elementary and secondary level, the sisters served primarily in administrative positions while lay women and men took their place in the classroom.

---

126   Following the completion of her term as Provincial Superior Sister Mary Francelia served as founding principal of Sacred Heart Elementary School in Ventura, a position she held for the next sixteen years (1980-1996). In 1996, Sister joined the staff of the A. F. International School of Languages for Foreign Students in Westlake, California where she taught advanced level courses in English to adults wishing to be licensed in the United States or to attend a North American university.

127   Sister Mary Joann (Joann Schlarbaum) entered the community in 1950 in Cleveland, Ohio. Following her profession in California in 1953 Sister taught in the elementary schools in St. Francis of Assisi, St. Helen, and St. Joan of Arc parishes. In 1958 Sister began her ministry of leadership first as Aspirant Mistress (1958-1970), then Junior Mistress (1975-1980) and finally Provincial Superior (1980-1992).

In the area of catechetical formation, the situation was much the same. Sisters now held the title Director of Religious Education for the parish. As such they planned the curriculum, enlisted the teachers and supervised the program rather than presented formal classroom instruction to children who did not attend parochial schools.

At the same time the community's continued response to the needs of the Church, especially in Los Angeles, resulted in a greater diversification of ministries. Now the sisters also served in the areas of adult spirituality and education, pastoral ministry, seminary training and evangelization. One sister also ministered in the National Institute of Transplantation at St. Vincent Hospital, Los Angeles, while another helped in the community dispensary in Jamalpur, India. Sisters also worked for the Archdiocese of Los Angeles itself as Religious Services Coordinator for the Department of Cemeteries and as Research Associate for the Department of Catholic Schools. Lastly, a sister directed the Caring Ministry at St. Lawrence of Brindisi Parish, while another was employed by the Department of Children and Family Services for the County of Los Angeles.

Unique perhaps among these new ministries was *Notre Dame Creations*. When exhibited at national conventions, Sister Rose Marie Tulacz's photographs of the world's natural beauty, in the form of cards and framed works, introduced the Congregation itself to a broader audience. At the same time such displays contributed to the community's ministry of evangelization and education, albeit in an indirect way.

This diversification of ministry, however, did not mean that the sisters abandoned their commitment to formal classroom instruction. In 1989 the sisters in California joined the members of the other three American provinces to launch the Notre Dame Educational Association (NDEA), a collaborative effort to reinforce the Congregation's influence on education. Sister Mary Immaculette Moose, Sister Mary Lisa Megaffin and Sister Gina Marie Blunck represented Rosa Mystica Province on the initial steering committee, which wrote the first by-laws and developed the organization's structure. In the ensuing years, the NDEA, promoted the Congregation's

Educational Cornerstones – *Dignity of the Teacher, Respect for the Individual Student, Thoroughness of Instruction and Centrality of Religion* – in a variety of ways. Among these was the production of a video for use in each of the community-owned schools.

As always the sisters worked closely with the lay men and women whom they encountered in their various ministries. However, the universal call to holiness emphasized by Vatican Council II reminded the sisters that among these individuals were persons who had developed a bond with the community that went beyond ministerial collaboration. Therefore, the sisters looked for ways to share their spirituality, life and ministry with these women and men who identified so closely with the charism of St. Julie Billiart. The result was the Associate Program.

The Associate Program

The first group of Associates

At this juncture there was no model within the Congregation for a program which would allow members of the laity to share in the community's spirituality. Therefore, in 1998, Sister Mary

Amy Hauck,[128] Sister Mary Regina Robbins, Sister Mary Francelia Klingshirn and Sister Mary Rebekah Kennedy formed a Core Committee in order to design such a program for the California province.

The result was a plan which essentially replicated the Rite of Christian Initiation for Adults (RCIA) used in the parishes in the Archdiocese. During a period of intentional formation, candidates would be introduced to the history, charism, spirit and mission of the Congregation. At the same time, they would also share the sisters' times of prayer, community life and ministry. At the conclusion of this formation period, the candidates would be admitted as Associates during a special Covenant Ceremony. The agreement made at this time would not carry the force of a vow or promise. Rather the relationship which the candidates assumed was essentially one of a mutual sharing of spirituality and did not involve financial obligations or participation in Congregational government.

The Core Committee brought these ideas together in a special book which included an explanation of the program itself as well as a description of privileges and responsibilities of Associates. They also developed an outline for the Formation Classes, and created an informational brochure. The sisters hoped to hold the initial Inquiry Meeting in the spring of 1999 so that the first Covenant Ceremony could take place on one of the feast days of St. Julie Billiart in the year 2000.

Accordingly the first Inquiry Days were held at Notre Dame Center, Thousand Oaks, on March 7 and at St. Helen's convent in South Gate on March 14, 1999. The program for both days included an explanation of the Associate Program, two presentations, the first entitled "Spirituality – The Heart of the Associate

---

128   Sister Mary Amy [Mary Louise Hauck] entered the Congregation in Thousand Oaks in 1968. Beginning in 1972, Sister taught at the following elementary schools: Our Lady of Perpetual Help, Downey; St. Paschal Baylon, Thousand Oaks, and St. Rose of Lima, Maywood. In 1980, Sister was named superior and principal at Notre Dame Academy, Los Angeles (1980-1987). In 1987 Sister Mary Amy was appointed Assistant Provincial and Superior at Notre Dame Center (1987-1992), and in 1992, Superior of Rosa Mystica Province (1992-2001).

Relationship;" the second, "The Privileges and Responsibilities of an Associate," and lastly, a description of the application process.

On Sunday, May 13, 2000, the feast of St. Julie Billiart, the first eleven women and men made their Covenant in the chapel at Notre Dame Center. During the brief ceremony each received a special pin which identified them as Associates of Notre Dame.

Providence House

In spite of the decrease in personnel, the attitude of the sisters in Rosa Mystica Province was optimistic particularly with regard to the future. During 1998-1999, the province leadership was looking for specific ways by which to implement the Directional Statement promulgated by the 1998 General Chapter. A study conducted by the Center for Applied Research in the Apostolate, indicated that their research showed that there was a window of opportunity for the acceptance of new members into religious life and that, if the community was not prepared to welcome them, that opportunity would be lost. Consequently, the Provincial Council, with the support of the sisters, decided to devise a definite plan of formation and to prepare a sister, both spiritually and theologically, to serve as Director of Formation. Since the section at Notre Dame Center which had formerly housed the novices and postulants had been converted into an assisted living unit, another site would have to be found.

Rather than locate the new House of Formation in the Thousand Oaks area, the Council decided to look for property in a neighborhood closer to Los Angeles and near colleges and universities. The sisters also wanted to establish the novitiate within a parish that would offer the novices and postulants the opportunity to participate in a vibrant parochial life and, at the same time, engage in various out-reach activities to the poor and marginalized. On November 1, 1999 the community closed negotiations for a four bedroom home in Long Beach, California.

Although the house itself was large, certain renovations were necessary in order to have space for a chapel, additional bedrooms and a bigger laundry and storage space. The sisters also wanted a larger community room and dining area as well as a garden that would be conducive to reflection. Accordingly work was begun in March 2000.

In the meantime, the sisters who would comprise the Providence House community lived at St. Rose of Lima convent in Maywood. Earlier that year Monsignor George Duran, pastor of St. Rose of Lima Parish, had been notified that the lack of personnel compelled the community to withdraw from the administration of his parochial school. Monsignor, however, had told the sisters they could continue to live in the convent as long as necessary. Furthermore, they were welcome to take whatever furnishings they needed for Providence House.

Despite the fact that the renovations on Providence House were not yet finished, October 19, 2000 was designated as Moving Day. The Annals noted:

> At approximately 5:10 p.m. the movers completed unloading the furniture from St. Rose of Lima Convent in Maywood. Although there were a number of details to be completed in our house, we were happy to find running water and our rooms equipped with beds! We continued unpacking boxes trying to make some order...but we knew it was not an overnight task. Many days [would be] required to make the house into our home.[129]

In 1999 when the community was planning the House of Formation, no young women had as yet expressed a desire to enter. Sister Mary Amy Hauck recalled:

> At the time we did not have someone knocking at the door. But I was struck by the line in the movie, *Field of Dreams*, "If you build it, they will come." So we formulated a program, chose a formator and located a place.

---

129   Annals, Providence House, 2000. ASNDTO.

Then Voila! Cristina Buczkowski [now Sister Cristina Marie] asked to enter."[130]

The Northridge Earthquake of 1994

For anyone living in Southern California, earthquakes are just a part of life. Even in 1933, when two Long Beach Earthquakes severely damaged both the convent and school at St. Matthias, the sisters never considered abandoning their ministries and returning to Ohio. They simply accepted the inconveniences which such a disaster brought and went on with their work.

The same attitude was apparent sixty years later, in 1994, when at 4:31 a.m. on Monday, January 14 1994, the Northridge Earthquake struck. Although its epicenter was in the San Fernando Valley, the effects were felt as far away as Thousand Oaks and West Los Angeles. The Pacific Earthquake Engineer Research Center in northern California reported "Estimates of more than $20 billion in property damage [made] this earthquake the costliest seismic disaster in U.S. history."[131]

In Thousand Oaks, the damage to Notre Dame Center was relatively minor. The Provincial House Annals recorded:

> When the Sisters [at Notre Dame Center] returned to their...rooms they found drawers jolted open and floors littered with books, papers and other moveable objects. Though there was no structural damage...there were cracks in the walls, bits of plaster that had broken from the corners of the walls, statues and other articles were broken...Not one thing, however, was askew in the chapel, no plants or pedestals overthrown.[132]

---

130   Sister Mary Amy [Hauck], Conversation with the author, October 18, 2000.
131   Pacific Earthquake Engineer Research (REER) Center, University of California, Berkeley, 2005.
132   Annals, Rosa Mystica Provincial House (Notre Dame Center), 1994, 1. ASNDTO.

At LaReina High School, though, the damage was more severe. In the classroom building the ceiling tiles had been disturbed. Because they contained asbestos, they would have to be replaced. In addition to the expense, it meant that the students could not use the rooms until the repairs were completed. Unfortunately at Notre Dame Academy in West Los Angeles the damage from the earthquake was more costly and extensive.

In both the elementary and high school buildings, the teachers found the familiar earthquake mess – books and papers on the floor, furniture tipped over, pictures askew. The convent, however, suffered major structural damage. Many of the bricks in the exterior veneer had cracked. The pillars on both the front and west porches had moved and the room above the side porch, once a porch as well, had pulled away from the main structure. In all the rooms plaster had fallen and the walls and ceilings had cracks. Worst of all, the support beams in the basement had shifted. This damage was compounded by the fact that the house itself was seventy years old and had never been retrofitted or renovated.

Since the damage was so extensive, the provincial leadership seriously considered razing the building. However, the house was regarded as a landmark in the area, so the decision was made to retain the exterior walls, gut the entire interior and, using the original footprint, erect a new more modern convent with sufficient bedrooms for all the sisters. At the same time, the elementary school would acquire space for a long-desired computer lab and music room.

This plan, however, was not as simple as it sounded. In order to gut the building, the house first had to be emptied. Therefore, the sisters went through the convent tagging various items. Some articles such as furniture, rugs, mattresses, and draperies as well as wood, metal and glass fixtures would be stored for future use. Other items would be sold in order to reduce the final cost; while still others, considered unsalvageable, would be discarded. By the end of November it was possible to stand in the second floor of the convent and look directly into the basement. In December, the re-construction began.

At the same time, the sisters living at Notre Dame Academy needed a place to stay. Two of the sisters moved to the convent at St. Francis of Assisi Parish and commuted to West Los Angeles each day. The remaining members of the community moved into the rooms which the aspirants had formerly occupied, in what was familiarly known as "The Villa."

Following the closure of the aspirant program in 1970, the preps' dormitories had been converted into private bedrooms for the sisters. The large central room was used chiefly for conversations and television viewing. When the sisters moved in, this room became both their dining and community room. Sister Mary LaReina Kelly, the local superior at the time, remembered:

> The only general room was the entrance section of the Villa. The portable TV had to be placed in the one general area. As a result anyone who wanted to come/go… most likely blocked the TV for those few minutes. If a visitor came, the same was true – stand and talk with others sitting in the common room. Anyone present instantly knew other's business so a sense of confidentiality had to prevail.
>
> A corner of the small room off the entrance became our eating area for breakfast and lunch. We had to use the high school cafeteria for supper and, although the sister cooks were very gracious, they found it challenging.
>
> The laundry was a washer/dryer combination with definite schedules for who could use it when. We had to go to a public Laundromat once a week for major laundry.
>
> On one level conditions were incredibly difficult; but because the sisters were committed to living this way, there was very little complaining. Naturally, tenseness arose at times, yet everyone "knew" what each other was experiencing emotionally and nothing was done on purpose. Charity ran high as the sisters understood the

variety of personalities and the need to make these living conditions succeed.[133]

In spite of the fact that the target date for the end of construction had been set for April 1995, work on the convent went on for nearly a year. It was mid-summer before the community could move back in. Finally on August 20, the sisters welcomed over 600 family and friends to an open house and blessing of their newly restored and renovated home.

With a Little Help from Our Friends

The cost of renovating Notre Dame Academy represented a major financial undertaking for Rosa Mystica Province. That the community was able to complete the renovations at Notre Dame Academy so successfully was due to the efforts of the recently established Development Office.

By 1990, the number of members in the province had dropped to 118. Of that number, only about 42% of the sisters were earning a full-time salary. Therefore, it quickly became apparent that the community needed to invite their families, friends, alumni and colleagues to become partners in their mission. As a result, in 1992, Sister Mary Kristin Battles (formerly Sister Mary Leslie) was appointed Director of Development.[134]

Among Sister's first tasks was to compile a database of potential benefactors. The fact that this tool was in place when the Northridge Quake struck enabled the community to begin fund raising on a more professional level.

Sister's efforts and those of her successors in publicizing the sisters' various ministries, organizing events such as Swing Into

---

133   Sister Mary LaReina Kelly, S.N.D., conversation with the author, December 23, 2009.
134   In the mid-1980s the province had launched a quarterly newsletter, "Vision and Challenge." The publication was designed not only to keep friends of the community in touch with the sisters but also to acquaint them with both the national and international dimensions of the Congregation.

Spring and writing grants have continued to support both the province's "Life and Ministry" and Retirement funds.

A Missionary Tradition

Support for the missions had always been a vital part of the sisters' ministry in California. From the onset, the elementary schools had actively participated in the missionary efforts of the Archdiocese itself through the Society for the Propagation of the Faith and the Holy Childhood Association. As members of the Province of Christ the King (1924 -1961), the sisters themselves had followed with keen interest the accounts from the provincial house in Cleveland describing the opening of the first convent in Jamalpur, India in 1949. Indeed, one of the members of the second group of pioneers, Sister Mary Freda Meyer, was stationed at Our Lady of Perpetual Help in Downey when she received her appointment to the new mission.[135]

Beginning in 1959, the sisters had also developed a special interest in the Congregation's mission in Papua New Guinea since sisters from the Province of Mary Immaculate in Toledo, Ohio frequently stopped in Los Angeles on their way to the new foundation.

. In 1972, the sisters added the first of a series of Mission Boutiques to the annual roast beef dinner and raffle. The sale offered not only a variety of home made bakery goods but also a wide selection of hand-crafted items and knitted goods, most of which were made by the sisters themselves. The proceeds from these sales were divided among the Congregation's missions in India, New Guinea, Indonesia and Brazil.

The sisters' commitment to the Church's missionary work, however, became even more pronounced when early in 1993,

---

135   Sister Mary Freda, the natural sister of Sister Mary Selma Meyer, S.N.D., had been stationed in California since 1947. During the next ten years two more sisters were missioned to India while stationed in California; Sister Mary Matilde Debesis in 1956 and Sister Mary Clarice (formerly Sister Mary Nathaniel) in 1960.

Sister Mary Amy Hauck invited the sisters to discern whether God was calling the province to support a mission in Uganda.

Buseesa, Kibaalei District, Uganda

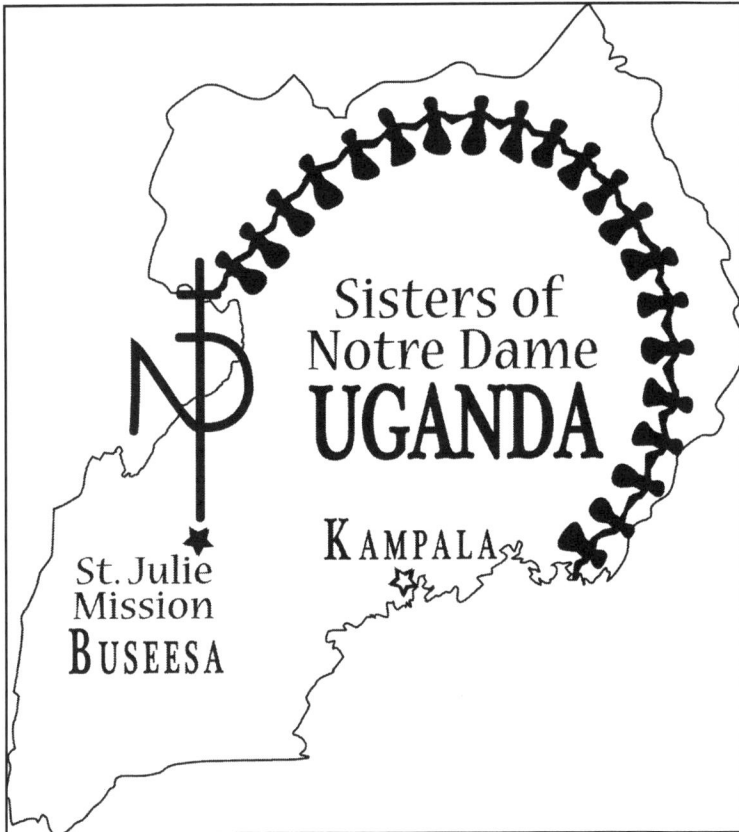

The possibility of a foundation in Uganda had first been suggested the previous autumn during the 1992 General Chapter. One afternoon, during a recess in the proceedings, Sister Mary Joell Overman, Superior General of the Congregation,[136] had

136   Sister Mary Joell (Overman) entered the Congregation in Covington, Kentucky in 1956. Sister received a Master's Degree in Hospital Administration from St. Louis University in 1969. She served as head of the Board of Directors of St. Charles

suggested that perhaps one or the other provinces might consider assuming responsibility for a mission in Africa.

The previous April Sister Mary Joell had received a letter from the Most Reverend Deogratias Byabazaire, Bishop of the Diocese of Hoima in Uganda, a country in the eastern region of Africa. The Bishop had written that it had been "the ardent desire of our diocese to have the witness, charisms and services of international missionary congregations within the diocese. At the moment, our diocese has little of this important aspect of church life."[137] In consequence, he invited the Congregation to come into Uganda in order to assist in the education of girls and women.

In a second letter, dated four months later, August 7, 1992, Bishop Deogratias had been more specific. He asked the Congregation to take over St. Cecily Secondary School for Girls, in Bukuumi, a city in the southern part of his diocese. Although the school had been established as an independent institution, a lack of finances and personnel had compelled it to merge with nearby St. Edward School for Boys. As a result, the education of the young women had suffered tremendously. The Bishop was anxious to restore the school.[138]

Sister Mary Joell informally passed on Bishop Deogratias' request to the Chapter delegates. After much prayer and discernment Sister Mary Amy Hauck and Sister Mary Margaret Droege, superior of the Province of the Immaculate Heart of Mary in Covington, Kentucky, suggested that their respective provinces might consider a joint venture. However, both provincials felt it was imperative to have a better understanding of

Nursing Home and St. Clare Medical Center as well as a member of the Board of St. Elizabeth Medical Center and Thomas More College, before being elected superior of the Immaculate Heart of Mary Province, Covington, Kentucky in 1983. Three years later Sister Mary Joell was elected eighth Superior General of the Sisters of Notre Dame (1986-1998).

137   Deogratias Byabazaire, Bishop of Hoima, Letter to Very Reverend Sr. Mary Joell Overman, SND, April 22, 1992. ASNDTO. The original is in the archives of the Generalate, Rome.
138   Deogratias Byabazaire, Bishop of Hoima, Letter to Very Reverend Sr. Mary Joell Overman, SND, August 7, 1992. ASNDTO. The original is in the archives of the Generalate, Rome.

both the conditions in East Africa as well as the needs of the diocese of Hoima itself before making a commitment.

Accordingly, on October 30, 1993, Sister Mary Joell and Sister Mary Amy met Sister Mary Margaret in Brussels.[139] The two provincials then flew to Uganda. During the following week, October 30 - November 7, the sisters traveled throughout the Hoima diocese in order to ascertain the extent of the Bishop's request.[140]

Sister Mary Amy and Sister Mary Margaret left Uganda on November 7 without making a specific commitment. Although both superiors strongly believed that their respective provinces were called to minister in Africa, they felt that their sisters were unfamiliar with the Ugandan culture. Moreover, the Congregation itself was not known in the area. As a result, the sisters did not believe that the community could solve the problems which St. Cecily Secondary School faced. They proposed beginning a model primary school instead.

Sister Mary Amy returned to California on November 12 filled with enthusiasm for the proposed mission and firmly convinced that God's providence was directing the endeavor. However, neither she nor Sister Mary Margaret felt they could move forward unless they had the support of the members of their respective provinces.

During the preceding months, however, Sister Mary Amy had spoken to her sisters about Bishop Deogratias' invitation, first informally during the annual Visitation and then at more formal gatherings at either Notre Dame Academy or Notre Dame Center. At the same time she asked the sisters to express their own thoughts concerning the proposed mission by completing a brief questionnaire.

In a letter to the community, dated March 8, 1993, Sister Mary Amy reported that, judging from her informal conversations with the sisters, "The response of the province [to the possibility of a mission in Uganda] has been overwhelmingly

---

139   Sister Mary Amy and the members of the Provincial Council were in Rome for an in-service with Sister Mary Joell and the members of the General Council.

140   Sister Mary Loretta Pastva, S.N.D. and Sister Mary Boaventura Jasper, S.N.D., *Vineyards in a Far Country: 1992-2007 Celebrating Fifteen Years of Notre Dame Presence in East Africa*. Generalate, Rome: The Sisters of Notre Dame, no date. 222. Cited hereinafter as Pastva, *Vineyards*.

positive."[141] In another letter, written in December 1993, Sister was more specific: "Of those Sisters completing the survey, 65% favored beginning a mission; 25% were opposed... [and] 10% were uncertain. Sister concluded:

> After considering the questionnaire and having received the encouragement and support of Sister Mary Joell and the provincial council, I believe the province response indicates that we go forth in our plans for our African mission.[142]

Sister Mary Amy later recounted that when it was time to tally the questionnaires, she felt she needed more than a simple majority if she were to proceed.

> At the time, we were about 100 professed Sisters in California. I had already told God that we needed more than 50% support; I needed 65% to make this happen. Sister Mary Kristin [Battles who was then Assistant Provincial] and I sat down on the floor of my office and sorted the responses into piles: yes, no, not certain. Finally Sister Kristin counted the YES responses: 65 Yes responses, on the dot! Does God not come through, or not?[143]

In a letter to Sister Mary Joell, dated December 25, 1993, Sister Mary Amy and Sister Mary Margaret jointly announced:

> We are happy to tell you that in each of our provinces the majority of sisters indicated their support for pursuing the establishment of the model primary school which we discussed with the bishop of Hoima.[144]

141   Sister Mary Amy [Hauck], Letter, March 8, 1993. ASNDTO.
142   Sister Mary Amy [Hauck], Letter, Christmas 1993. ASNDTO. Cited hereinafter as Letter, Christmas 1993. ASNDTO.
143   Conversation with the author, January 22, 2010.
144   Pastva, *Vineyards.* 222.

On January 26, 1994 Sister Mary Amy met Sister Mary Joell and Sister Mary Margaret in Toledo in order to clarify, to some degree, the issues of governance, personnel and finance. At the same time, Sister hoped that it would be possible to formulate a tentative timeline for the project.

Missioned to Uganda

Sr. Jane Marie McHugh (CA), Sr. Mary Delrita Glaser (Cov),
Sr. Mary Janet Stamm (Cov), and Sr. Margaret Mary Scott (CA)

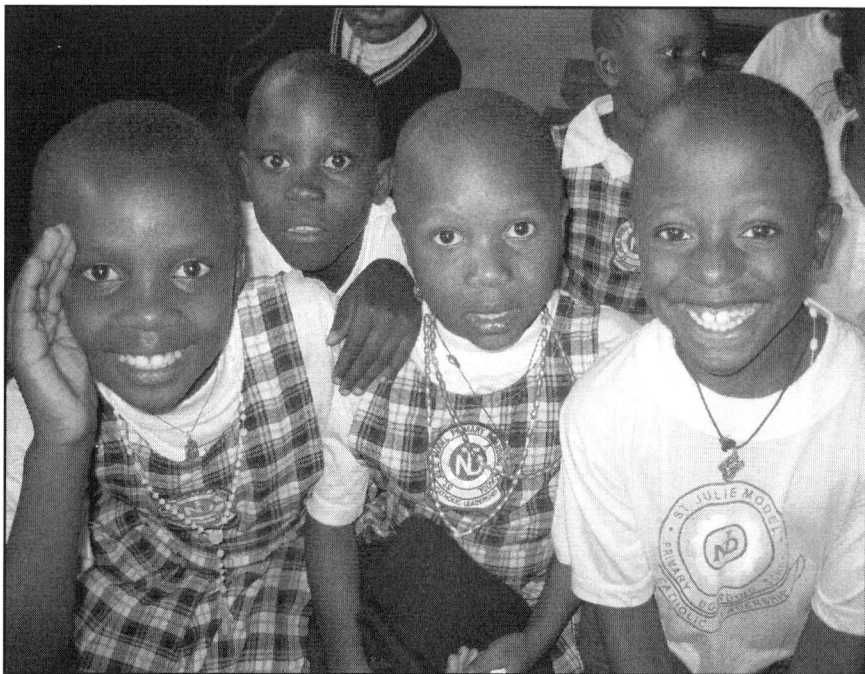

Ugandan Students

Since December 1993, the sisters of the Rosa Mystica Province had been discerning their own personal call to Africa. In the same letter in which she had announced the members' readiness to respond positively to Bishop Deogratias' invitation, Sister Mary Amy wrote: "Six sisters indicated their willingness to minister in Uganda now. Four sisters indicated that they would like to go after they fulfilled other family and ministry commitments."[145] Finally, at a province gathering on the Feast of the Annunciation, 1994, Sister announced the names of the two sisters from California who, together with Sister Mary Janet Stamm and Sister Mary Delrita Glaser from Immaculate Heart of Mary Province in Covington, would begin Rosa Mystica's mission in Uganda: Sister Jane Marie McHugh (formerly Sister Mary Teressa) and Sister Margaret Mary Scott.

Now that the leadership of the two provinces had formally accepted Bishop Deogratias' invitation, planning and preparation for the new venture began in earnest. In May 1994, Sister Mary

---

145   Letter, Christmas, 1993. ASNDTO.

Amy was in Covington for five days of meetings with Sister Mary Joell and Sister Mary Margaret and her council.[146] On October 12, 1994 the two provincials returned to Uganda to select a site and purchase the necessary land. At the same time, they intended to draw up the blue prints for a convent and arrange for digging a well. After meeting with members of the diocesan leadership as well as with the pastors/catechists from the neighboring parishes, Bishop Deogratias and his secretary, Father Charles, drove the two sisters to a number of possible sites. "Buseesa was the last," Sister Mary Amy recalled, "and we sort of fell in love with the place."

> It was poor; not even the Ugandans wanted to go into the Kibaale area. We knew we could make a difference. The people were warm and welcoming. The diocese had enough land there so we could expand over time. The countryside was beautiful.[147]

In the meantime, Sister Jane Marie and Sister Margaret Mary were preparing for their ministry in Uganda. In September 1994 the two sisters flew to Covington to meet Sister Mary Janet and Sister Mary Delrita and their families and, at the same time, to become acquainted with the sisters and the spirit of the Covington province.[148] From Kentucky, the four missionaries traveled to Chicago, Illinois in order to participate in the month-long Maryknoll Cross-Cultural Training Program. Lastly, the sisters had the opportunity to meet sisters in both the Chardon and Toledo provinces who had been missionaries in India, and Papua New Guinea.

Back in California, Sister Jane Marie and Sister Margaret Mary took classes in Auto Mechanics and Off-the-Road 4-Wheel Driving at Ventura City College although, as Sister Jane Marie later remarked: "But nothing here could adequately prepare us for the roads of the Kibaale District." Of special value for both California's missionaries-to-be were the days which they spent

---

146   In March 1995, from the 2nd to the 6th, Sister Mary Margaret came to California for the same purpose.
147   Conversation with the author, December 11, 2009.
148   Sister Mary Janet and Sister Mary Delrita made a similar visit to Southern California in February of the following year.

with Dr. Francine Bradley, Professor and Chairperson of the Department of Avian Sciences at the University of California at Davis in northern California.[149]

At the university, Dr. Bradley gave Sister Jane Marie and Sister Margaret Mary one-to-one tutoring in the care of chickens and other fowl, from egg to evisceration. In addition, she arranged for another professor to instruct them in the French Intensive Method of Farming and in the "art" of composting; that is, transforming garbage into fertilizer, The two sisters also visited a goat farm in order to learn how to milk a goat and to make goat cheese and spent time with another professor whose field of expertise was East African history and culture.

Sister Jane Marie and Sister Margaret Mary were slated to leave for Uganda in the summer of 1995. The Missioning Ceremony and Farewell took place in the chapel at Notre Dame Center on Sunday, July 9, 1995. At the conclusion of a festive brunch, Sister Mary Amy presented each sister with a replica of the Coesfeld Cross which she had previously received from Sister Mary Joell with the suggestion that perhaps she would like to use them "as missioning crosses for the…sisters being missioned to Uganda."[150] Following the presentation, Father Daniel O'Sullivan, pastor of Sacred Heart Parish, Ventura, Father Peter Banks, O.F.M., Cap, pastor of St. Lawrence of Brindisi Parish, and Father John Higson, a relative by marriage to Sister Jane Marie, concelebrated the Mass for the Spread of the Gospel. The Eucharistic Liturgy was followed by a special blessing for the two missionaries and a luncheon and reception for their friends and families.

Land of the Ugandan Martyrs

The beginnings of St. Julie Model Primary School and Convent in Buseesa were, in some ways, much like the opening of other Notre Dame schools and convents in Southern California.

---

149   Dr. Bradley was a former student of Sister Mary Josanne Fury, S.N.D. and a graduate of LaReina High School, Thousand Oaks.
150   Cited in Pastva, *Vineyards.* 226.

Sister Jane Marie and Sister Margaret Mary arrived in Entebbe on Thursday, July 13, 1995, but spent the first two weeks familiarizing themselves with the Kibaale District, the diocese of Hoima and the capital city of Kampala. In addition to making a formal visit to Cardinal Wamala Emmanuel, who gave them two relics of the Ugandan Martyrs for their convent chapel, and to the Apostolic Nuncio, Archbishop Christophe Pierre, the sisters visited several primary schools in Hoima as well as the eight parishes whose children would eventually attend the primary school. It was not until July 21 that the sisters were able to move into their new home.

St. Julie Convent was built on a hillside overlooking the gently rolling hills of Buseesa and Bejuni. It was a large brick structure laid out in a rectangle with large open courtyard in the center. But only about 1/2 of the house – the guest block, the upper kitchen block and part of the dining room/sitting room/main kitchen/laundry block – were completed. Moreover, the foundation for the main wing which would contain the parlor and community rooms, the chapel, bathrooms, and individual bedrooms for the sisters had not even been dug.

As sisters before them had done, the four sisters quickly adapted the existing rooms to other uses. A small storeroom in the guest wing was converted into a temporary chapel while another storeroom and two of the guest rooms became bedrooms for the sisters. This arrangement lasted until December 1996 when the convent wing was finally finished.

However, the other challenges which the sisters faced were unique. Among the first difficulties was the need for water. St. Julie Convent did not have a well. As a result, the sisters quickly learned that drinking water was a precious commodity. Sister Jane Marie wrote:

> Instead of merely turning on the tap, we pray for rain which is collected in a storage tank, manually pumped to the house lines, boiled [for at least twenty minutes], cooled, filtered drop by drop and finally poured into litre bottles.[151]

---

151   [Sister Jane Marie McHugh] Letter to Sisters families and friends, August 10, 1995.

When the sisters arrived, the rainy season had not begun so the water tanks were empty. Fortunately two heavy rains within the next few days filled the tanks to the brim.

A second necessity was food. Although the local people had welcomed them with gifts of fruits, eggs, vegetables and even a live chicken, the sisters quickly discovered that they needed to go shopping. Sister Margaret Mary recounted:

> Low on food supply, [we] heard of a marketplace every Saturday at the village on the next ridge. Without a guide, [Sister Mary Delrita and Sister Jane Marie] hiked down the valley and up – a 45 minute trip. Instead of produce [they] found people sampling the local brew. Banana beer anyone?[152]

Therefore, the following day the sisters, accompanied by Father Mugisa Aloysius, made the six hour round trip to Kampala. As Sister Mary Janet described it, the experience was an exhausting one.

> There are vendors all along the streets, large open air markets, many small shops and a few larger ones like Star Market. Prices vary and especially in the open markets are determined by who the purchaser is and how much the vendor thinks he can get for his wares. Skill in bargaining is called for to negotiate a good price.[153]

Almost immediately upon their arrival in the capital, the sisters met a nineteen-year-old Ugandan young man, Patrick, who offered to do their shopping. At first the sisters resisted the idea, but finally gave in. So Patrick and his network of "boys" ran around taking care of their needs. Although Patrick haggled for the best possible prices on the sisters' behalf, the purchases were still expensive.

ASNDTO.
152   [The] Buseesa SNDs, Letter to Sister Mary Amy, August 28, 1995, ASNDTO. This letter was a compilation of articles written by Sister Jane Marie, Sister Margaret Mary, Sister Mary Janet and Sister Mary Delrita for a Ugandan newsletter.
153   [Sister Mary Janet Stamm], Ibid. 4. ASNDTO.

In Star Market prices are displayed on or near the items, but things are very expensive, especially things that Westerners might buy like Kellogg's Cornflakes which costs $9.00 a box in USA money. We paid $50.00 for a simple medium-size plastic cooler which we needed to carry meat in when we [make] the long trip to Buseesa.[154]

Another important source of food for the sisters was the convent garden. One day a local woman knocked at the door and informed the sisters that she had come to help them start their garden. Sister Margaret Mary wrote:

Theresa helped us clear and level the ground, prepare three plots about a metre wide with a path space in between. Two plots have beans and peas and one will be a seed bed to nurture seedlings. Preparation of this bed involves 1) covering the bed with straw then setting fire to it to kill pests, 2) blending in the ashes, 3) planting seeds and covering [them] with grass, 4) building a little thatched shelter where seedlings grow to transplant size...

Our gardens are not free from invasion. Some neighboring goats found their way here.... One morning, a whole family of rats scampered through our patch. We will burn the maize they feed on as well as the elephant grass that is their hideout. Then we hope to get a little kitten to keep the rodents permanently scared away.[155]

Since Ugandan food was rather monotonous and bland, the sisters also planted a small herb garden containing parsley, anise, chervil, peppers and cilantro in order to add a little spice to their diet.

By mid autumn, the sisters were eager to begin their ministry. In early October Sister Jane Marie volunteered to teach at St. Andrea, a government primary school down the road from the convent. Shortly afterward Sister Mary Janet joined her and, by the beginning of the 1996 school term, Sister Mary Delrita and Sister Margaret Mary were there as well. For the next fifteen months,

154   [Sister Mary Janet Stamm], Ibid. 4. ASNDTO.
155   [Sister Margaret Mary Scott] Ibid. 3-4. ASNDTO.

Sister Jane Marie taught seventh level English and math; Sister Mary Delrita, sixth level English; Sister Margaret Mary, fifth level science and Sister Mary Janet, fourth level English and religion. During the December holiday break, they also added a special class to prepare the P-7 students for the Primary Leaving Exam.

Once again the conditions under which they would work were very different from those in the United States. Sister Mary Delrita described one of the sisters' first visits to the school.

> St. Andrea consisted of three buildings.
>
> The first building has three rooms, one for each grade, P-1, P-2 and P-3....Each classroom is the same: mud daub walls, window openings without glass, no door, earthen floor. On the front wall a smooth board painted black gives the teacher a place to write with chalk. The children sit on benches – about 9 on a bench — and have long narrow tables for their copy books.
>
> From the three primary classes we moved to the next building where levels 6 and 7 have class. The building is older. The earth floor is no longer even and the rusted tin roof is held in place with stones and tree limbs laid across it. But the children had better desks and only sat three together...
>
> Finally we crossed the play area to the 3rd building where the 4th and 5th grades have class. This structure also had a leaky tin roof and in P-4 the students have no desks or tables [and] only a part of the class has bench seats. The rest sit on bricks neatly placed 2 or three together.[156]

The sisters' ministry at St. Andrea lasted until December of the following year, 1996, at which time preparations for building St. Julie Model Primary School were well underway.[157]

---

156   [Sister Mary Delrita Glaser], Ibid. 11. ASNDTO.
157   In addition to teaching at St. Andrea, Sister Jane Marie, Sister Mary Delrita and Sister Mary Janet taught English conversation classes to about twenty women from the district.

St. Julie Model Primary School

St. Julie School

As soon as the construction of the convent was finished, the sisters turned their attention to opening St. Julie Model Primary School. Once the site had been chosen, the official ground breaking took place on September 11, 1996 and the work began. Sister Jane Marie and Sister Mary Janet visited the site daily to talk to the foreman and to make sure that everything was progressing as they wished.

By spring 1997 Sister Jane Marie, who had been appointed head teacher or principal, was ready to begin the formal application process. Prior to this, however, the four sisters had done extensive ground work to insure the success of the school. Sister Jane Marie had begun by surveying the head teachers in the diocese's boarding schools to determine best practices. In addition, she had also spoken with the pastors of the nine feeder parishes, including Buseesa at a deanery meeting.[158]

---

158   At this meeting, the pastors were adamant that the word "model" should be included in the name of the school in order to distinguish St. Julie's from other pri-

The sisters were also anxious to support local vocational schools. Sister Jane Marie made arrangements with the Munteme Technical School in Kakindo to build the students' desks and stools. Likewise the following year, the girls at the Dominican School in neighboring Kakumiro were contracted to sew the school uniforms.

In late April 1997, Sister Jane Marie and Sister Mary Janet visited each of the eight feeder parishes[159] to introduce the school to the members of the Parish Councils and to convince them to entrust their village children to them. For the most part the parochial leadership were teachers or catechists who either worked in the parish itself or in the outlying stations or were employed by the nearby hospitals. Since there were no primary boarding schools in the Kibaale District and the students of the local government-sponsored schools seldom passed the Primary Leaving Exam or achieved higher than a six (the grades are 1 through 9 with 1 being the best) St. Julie Model Primary School represented an undreamed of opportunity for the village children.

Finally on February 2, 1998, classes began for 41 students, four or five from each of the feeder parishes.[160] Although in many ways, St. Julie Model Primary School was unique among the schools in Rosa Mystica Province, there was at least one thing that was the same.

When the sisters toured the school the day before its opening to make sure everything was ready, workmen were still in sight and debris and left-over construction materials were stacked in the halls, classrooms and dormitories. Sister Jane Marie hurried after the foreman urging him to get everything cleaned up: "The children will be here tomorrow! This has to be done!"

---

mary schools. They also insisted the school charge definite fees.

159   In addition to Buseea, the other parishes in the Kibaale District were Kahunde, Bukumi, Bujuni, Kalindo, Mahorro, Magalike, Kagadi and Kakumiro.

160   Sister Jane Marie had agreed to accept the four or five children in each parish who scored highest on the entrance exam so that each parish would be equally represented.

Los Angeles, A City of Diversity

California has always been an ethnically diverse state. The Gold Rush of 1849 lured Yankee Americans into an area originally colonized by Spain and Mexico. After them came the Chinese as well as African Americans, especially from the South, looking for jobs on the railroads. The religious persecutions in Mexico in the early twentieth century brought a resurgence of immigration from the states south of California's border while the fall of Saigon in 1975 flooded the region with refugees from Vietnam and other parts of Asia. Today nearly one-third of all foreign-born persons in the United States live in California. Los Angeles County contains within itself numerous cultural enclaves: Chinatown, Little Tokyo, Little Saigon, Korea Town, Filipino Town, Little Armenia, to name only a few.

The city-wide celebration of such events as *Cinco de Mayo*, the Chinese New Year and Nisei Week Japanese Festival drew attention to the multiplicity of national traditions within Los Angeles itself. Therefore, when the 1992 General Chapter articulated its goals: *personal conversion, forming communities of interdependence and action for the poor,* the sisters in Rosa Mystica Province were eager to find ways to expand this awareness, especially with regard to the cultural and ethnic diversity that existed within the Congregation itself. At the same time, they wanted to find ways to identify more closely with the economically poor.

Out-Reach Experience in Brazil

In 1993 the province leadership voted to explore the possibility of a summer program in which the sisters would visit the Provinces of Passo Fundo and Canoas in Brazil. The purpose of the experience was outlined in a letter to the sisters of the province, dated April 15, 1993.

The purpose of the program would be to provide those who participate with:

- a global and international awareness, particularly of SND internationality
- a first-hand experience of other cultural and economic world living
- an opportunity to share the lives of the poor with whom our sisters minister
- the occasion to see in action the faith-life of the impoverished in Brazil
- the assimilation, in some small way, of our Sisters' involvement with the very poor of Brazil
- the openness to personal conversion as a way of life
- living more simply
- an experience which provokes a change of perspective in every aspect of our lives.[161]

Accordingly, in 1993, Sister Betty Mae Bienlein (formerly Sister Mary Jorese) spent a month visiting Rio de Janeiro, Brasilia, Passo Fundo, Canoas and the province's missions in Acre.

The following summer, Sister returned to Brazil, this time accompanied by Sister Mary Frances Wahl. During their month-long stay the two sisters, together with a sister from each of the other provinces in the United States, visited the provincial houses in Canoas and Passo Fundo as well as the sisters' various ministries in Carazinho, Nao-Me-Toque, San Jose and Ibiruba. Since one of the purposes of the Out-Reach experience was to let the visitors see the faith-filled life of the impoverished, the sisters also toured various *favelas* in Canoas. as well as an encampment of people fighting for agricultural land and two clinics operated by the sisters, both in Passo Fundo.

Unfortunately several difficulties were inherent in this experience. The principal one was scheduling. Since Brazil was in the Southern Hemisphere, July and August were winter months during which the sisters in Passo Fundo were in school. However, in the Northern Hemisphere, July and August were part of the summer vacation, the only time when the sisters in the United States were free to travel. As a result, it was hard to identify sisters

161   Sister Mary Amy [Hauck], Letter to the Sisters, April 15, 1993. ASNDTO.

in Brazil who could act as guides or translators since their North American guests were not fluent in Portuguese.

Moreover, because the program was to be a reciprocal one, the superiors hoped the sisters from Brazil could spend time in the United States. However, because of the difference in seasons the sisters were able to visit the American provinces only during the months of December and January when the sisters in the United States were in school. Unfortunately these problems could not be easily resolved. Consequently, the program was not repeated.

The following year, 1995, the sisters were offered another opportunity to experience the internationality of the Congregation as well as to explore its rich heritage when the province initiated the Congregational Pilgrimage.

Congregational Pilgrimage

In 1992, Sister Mary Joann Schlarbaum's term as provincial came to an end. Subsequently, Sister Mary Joell had invited her successor, Sister Mary Amy Hauck, and the members of the new Provincial Council to come to Rome in October 1993 for an in-service with the General Council. Prior to these meetings, the sisters had had the opportunity to visit many of the places in Germany and Holland associated with the early history of the Congregation. The trip had made such an impression upon the sisters that the Council wanted to make it possible for other members of the province to have a similar experience.

Accordingly the following year the General Council in Rome opened negotiations with the European provincials on behalf of the Province of Rosa Mystica in order to ascertain if a similar pilgrimage to Germany and Holland were possible. The result was that in the summer of 1994 any sister who was in good health and felt she was able to withstand a month of intense travel was invited to apply to participate in what became known as the Congregational Pilgrimage.

After approximately six months of special prayer together with the study of the history of the provinces which they would visit, the first four pilgrims left the United States on March 20, 1995. The sisters traveled first to Germany – to Vechta, then

Coesfeld and ultimately Mulhausen. From there, they drove to Teglen in the Netherlands and then to Namur, Belgium to visit the Motherhouse of the Sisters of Notre Dame de Namur and the grave of St. Julie Billiart. Finally on March 31, 1995 the pilgrims arrived in Rome in time to celebrate Holy Week and Easter with the sisters at the Generalate before returning to Los Angeles.

Two years later, in 1997, the sisters from California were joined by sisters from the province of Mary Immaculate, Toledo and Immaculate Heart of Mary, Covington. In 2000, the sisters in the United States reciprocated the hospitality of the European provinces by hosting a similar pilgrimage for sisters from Mulhausen, Coesfeld and Teglen. As one of the sisters commented: "You came to Europe to see the roots, so we wanted to come to the United States to see the fruit."

While the Out-Reach Experience to Brazil and the Congregational Pilgrimage impacted a comparatively small number of the sisters, the 1996 General Conference, which was held in California, made all the sisters in Rosa Mystica Province more aware of the internationality of the Congregation.

General Conference of 1996

Sisters gather in Santa Barbara

The purpose of the Conference was to set the theme and agenda for the 1998 General Chapter. Sister Maria Monica Kim, the newly appointed superior of the Province of Our Lady of Peace, Korea, and her predecessor, Sister Marie Raphael Kang, were the first delegates to arrive. These sisters were followed by the Assistants General, Sister Margaret Mary Gilmore and Sister Anne Marie Robinson, on July 28, 1996, and shortly afterwards by Sister Mary Joell, and the remaining members of the general and provincial governments from Europe, Asia, Brazil and the United States.

The General Conference officially opened on Monday, August 5, with a special Eucharistic Liturgy in the chapel at Notre Dame Center in which all of the sisters of the province were invited to participate. The internationality of the Congregation was high-lighted by the presence of the flags of the thirteen nations in which the community ministered at that time as well as by the General Intercessions which were offered in the various languages spoken in the Congregation.

Although the succeeding days were taken up with meetings, presentations and a workshop by Reverend David L. Fleming, S.J., current editor of the quarterly *Review for Religious*, the sisters-hostesses found time to show their guests some of the beauty and history of Southern California. A bus tour of Los Angeles on Saturday, August 3 took the delegates into such diverse areas of the city as Beverly Hills, Hollywood, Chinatown, Olvera Street, Watts and Skid Row. A second tour the following Saturday, August 10, gave them the chance to visit the missions in Santa Barbara and Ventura as well as some of the other sights along the Pacific Coast.

Besides opportunities to sight-see, the conference participants were able to become more familiar with the sisters' lifestyle in California through special pre-arranged visits known as Hospitality Nights. On each of these Nights (August 7 and 12, 1996) the delegates shared Evening Prayer and supper with the sisters at the various convents in the province and had the chance to learn more about the ministries at that particular affiliation. Finally, a Western Style Barbeque on Saturday evening, August

17, complete with cowboy hats and bandanas, as well as instructions in the art of Line-Dancing, added a western flavor to the General Conference.

For the sisters of Rosa Mystica Province, the two weeks spent with the participants in the General Conference served to reinforce the diversity in language, culture and ministry which characterized the Congregation. For Sister Maria Mechtilde Kotterik, General Assistant for Germany at the time, the Conference was a time "to understand each other much better...to see [the sisters] in their places [of ministry] rather than to just read about them." Reflecting on her experience of the General Conference fifteen years later, Sister wrote: "I learned to understand a new culture and history. Still I am grateful for the hospitality and love in Provincial House and in the affiliations... I got to see so many beautiful things – walking in the ocean, sand sculptures in Thousand Oaks, a new parish church in Camarillo with the Baptismal Font in the back. All the events [of the Conference] are still very vital in my mind and heart."[162]

Reflecting on the experience Sister Mary Amy Hauck said:

> The General Conference was one of the best things that happened to our province. Every sister was able to connect with sisters from every country that had an ND presence. It broke open our world to the blessings and challenges of internationality. The hard work and united effort and love of each of our sisters made the experience come alive. It was one of our finest hours![163]

---

162   Sister Maria Mechtilde Kotterik, S.N.D, Letter to the author, November 2009.
163   Sister Mary Amy [Hauck]. Conversation with the author. 2009.

A Jubilee of Gratitude

***Sr. Mary Joan Schlotfeldt leads the entrance procession for the
Eucharistic Liturgy for the province celebration of the
sesquicentennial of the congregation***

A large white tent covered the front parking area of Notre
Dame Center on Sunday, August 13, 2000. In it more than 700
people – family members, former sisters, Associates, students,
colleagues, civic officials, and friends – gathered for a special

Eucharistic Liturgy celebrated by The Right Reverend Thomas J. Curry, Bishop of the Santa Barbara Region, assisted by sixteen priests and five deacons. The event was a double celebration: the sesquicentennial of the founding of the Congregation itself and the seventy-fifth anniversary of the sisters' arrival in California.

Outwardly the life style of the community had changed considerably since the first eleven sisters arrived in Los Angeles eager to open schools in Huntington Park and Watts. Nevertheless the qualities instilled by the first eleven sisters and nurtured by the women who followed them – a spirit of prayer, fidelity to a simple life-style, love of community, openness to the Spirit, trust in God's providence and loyalty to the Congregation and to the Church – are still apparent in the lives of the sisters of the Province of Rosa Mystica in California today.

Twenty-five years earlier, August 30, 1974, the sisters in California had gathered at St. Lawrence of Brindisi Parish for a special Eucharistic Liturgy followed by a picnic lunch celebrating the same anniversary. At that time three of the pioneer sisters, Sister Mary Balbina, Sister Mary Sirana and Sister Mary Walburge, were still active members of the province.[164] Shortly afterward, Sister Mary Sirana shared her thoughts about the sisters' ministry in California. The sentiments, paraphrased slightly, which Sister expressed then are still true today:

> I am filled with pride for what has been accomplished by our Notre Dame community….I am proud of our first sisters who kindled and nurtured the fire and who are an inspiration to those who [have] followed; proud of the scores of …sisters who are ministering under ever increasing challenges, who are doing splendid work for the church of Los Angeles. I am filled with gratitude to God for his providential care of our community and in particularly our Rosa Mystica Province. The fire enkindled by our pioneer sisters has grown and spread. It continues to warm, to enlighten, to strengthen and to comfort thousands of souls. "How good is the good God." To him be glory and praise forever.[165]

---

164   Sister Mary Sirana Kirchner died on November 23, 1977; Sister Mary Walburge Schmitt, on March 3, 1980, and Sister Mary Balbina Hagedorn, on July 11, 1986.

165   Wittenburg, House, 129. ASNDTO.

Province photo, 1995

Epilogue

Sister Mary Amy Hauck's term as provincial superior came to an end in the fall of 2001. On November 25, 2001, Sister Mary Kristin Battles (formerly Sister Mary Leslie) was installed as the sixth superior of Rosa Mystica Province.[166]

During the next ten years, 2000 – 2010, the sisters in California faced many of the same issues that concerned other religious communities in the United States at that time. Chief among these was the continued decrease in personnel together with the diminishment of financial resources, especially as a result of the economic crisis which had begun in 2002. Sister Mary Kristin and her council, however, decided to adopt a proactive stance to meet these challenges. Accordingly throughout Sister's nine years of leadership, the sisters of the province worked not only with various consultants but also among themselves to develop long range strategies and to identify specific areas to which they wished to devote their time and energies.

The decrease in membership could not help but impact the schools. Beginning in the 1980s, the community had gradually withdrawn from the various parochial schools in both the Diocese of Oakland and the Archdiocese of Los Angeles.[167] By the end of

---

166   Sister Mary Kristin (Leslie Battles) entered the community in Thousand Oaks, California in 1964. After a successful ministry in education as both teacher and administrator, Sister was appointed Assistant Provincial in 1992. In 2001, she was named Provincial Superior of the California province. On November 23, 2010, Sister Mary Kristin was elected tenth Superior General of the Sisters of Notre Dame.

167   The sisters had withdrawn from St. Leo School in 1972. However, this was due to the intention of the State of California's Division of Highways to build the Century Freeway the construction of which would bisect St. Leo Parish. As a result, the

the 2009-2010 school year, no sister of Rosa Mystica Province was ministering in any of the schools with whom the community had had a long and fruitful history.[168]

Concurrently the sisters took steps to insure the viability of the province's three community-owned institutions – Notre Dame Academy Elementary School, Notre Dame Academy and La Reina High School – and to preserve the Congregation's spirit, charism and mission for a time when no Sister of Notre Dame would be available to act as principal. In the spring of 2003, the Provincial Leadership began to explore the possibility of a new governance structure for each of the schools.

By 2005-2006 all three institutions had adopted a new administrative configuration: President, Principal and Board of Trustees.[169] On July 1, 2005, Sister Marie Paul Grech assumed the responsibilities of President of Notre Dame Academy, Los Angeles with Joan Tyhurst as principal. On the following October 25, the new board of governance, the Board of Trustees, was formally inducted at the Academy's annual Family Mass.

At the same time Sister Mary LaReina Kelly became President of Notre Dame Academy Elementary School and La Reina High School. Kathleen Nocella was named principal of Notre Dame; Cecilia Coe, principal of La Reina High School.

This arrangement was altered slightly. Beginning in September 2008, Nancy Coonis, former principal of St. Mathias High School, Huntington Park, and then Superintendent for Secondary Schools for the Archdiocese of Los Angeles, became President of Notre Dame Academy (Elementary and High School). The Boards of Trustees of both institutions were merged into one.

---

parish itself was suppressed. Ironically, the freeway itself was not constructed for nearly 20 years.

168   Several sisters were still engaged in formal classroom ministry at St. Dominic Parish School in Eagle Rock, St. Jude the Apostle School in Westlake and St. Hedwig School in Orange. However, the community's relationship with these parishes was different than in previous years since there was no commitment to provide teachers for these schools beyond the individual sisters' annual Agreement for Services.

169   A necessary part of this new organization was the incorporation of each school as a separate not-for-profit entity. This was finalized in 2007.

Sister Mary LaReina Kelly continued to serve as President of La Reina High School.

Shortly after the adoption of the new governance structure, the Boards of Trustees at both institutions – Notre Dame Academy and La Reina High School – initiated a strategic planning process which would insure their respective institutions' viability and fidelity to the community's educational heritage, charism and mission during the coming years.[170]

Although the number of sisters lessened, the first decade of the new century was one of enthusiasm and energy. Outreach to the poor has long been a tradition in Rosa Mystica Province. Even before the challenge of Vatican Council II calling for option to the poor, the sisters as individuals had reached out in various ways to the economically, intellectually and emotionally poor. In mid-decade, however, the sisters endeavored to make their presence as a Congregation more visible in the area of social justice within the Archdiocese of Los Angeles.

One of the issues that was of growing concern in the Los Angeles area was that of human trafficking. In 2006, in partnership with the Coalition Against Slavery and Trafficking (CAST), the province provided a house for the organization to use as a shelter for women victims of trafficking. In addition, the sisters themselves volunteered as supervisors, house mothers and hotline operators.

This same decade was also a time of growth both within the province itself and in Uganda. In 2005, Providence House in Long Beach was named the site of the combined United States novitiate. On July 30 and 31, four novices from the other three American provinces joined Sister Valerie Marie Roxburgh at Providence House. In 2007, and again in 2010, the sisters welcomed young women from the Chardon, Toledo and Covington provinces to California for their canonical year of formation under the direction of Sister Mary Kathleen Burns.

---

170   Since the fall of 2005, members of Rosa Mystica Province had also been active members of the national Sponsorship Committee whose purpose was to address the issue of lay leadership training for the community-owned schools.

The Associate Program also continued to expand. By the time the Associates celebrated their tenth anniversary in 2010, 70 men and women had made their covenant as Associates of Notre Dame.[171] Moreover, the Associates themselves had begun to assume an active role in the program by participating in the formation process, giving retreats both for themselves as well as others and sponsoring outreach activities, principally in Ventura County.

At Notre Dame Center, Notre Dame Learning Center opened on September 6, 2005 in what had originally been the classroom unit. Beginning with eighteen three and four year old boys and girls, the enrollment reached thirty-six children by the fall of 2009, in spite of the severe economic crisis impacting the United States at the time. It was in Uganda, however, that expansion was most apparent.

St. Julie Model Primary School had opened on February 2, 1998. With each succeeding year, a new grade level was added so that by 2006 the school had a P1- P7 configuration and the school enrollment was at capacity As the first class of primary school students neared graduation in December 2002, the sisters had already initiated plans for a secondary school so that the young women could continue their education under the auspices of the Sisters of Notre Dame. Notre Dame Academy Senior Secondary School opened in February 2003. By 2006, the four levels of this school, too, were complete.

The physical plant in Buseesa especially reflected this growth. The sisters' convent had been completed in 1996. Between 2001 and 2007, a science building and an administration building for the secondary school plus more classroom blocks had been added. In addition, a multipurpose building, which would be shared by both the primary and secondary students as well as used for various civic activities, had been erected. Because both St. Julie Model Primary School and Notre Dame Academy Senior Secondary School were boarding institutions, the plant also

---

171   Of this number, two members were deceased and one member had entered the community itself.

included dormitories for the students and housing for the lay faculty, staff and volunteers as well as dining and kitchen blocks.

Since the Buseesa site had to provide food not only for the sisters but also for the students and teachers, besides the convent garden, there were two large farms, one at Buseesa and a second at Mugarama. Among the crops grown there were avocados, pumpkins, pineapples, coffee and sweet potatoes. Since the sisters were determined that the students also had a balanced and varied diet, the livestock included cows, pigs, chickens, rabbits and turkeys.

Managing these farms as well as the need for teachers, house mothers and other staff members for the two schools meant that the lives of the people of Buseesa gradually improved through the payment of regular salaries. In 2009, a micro-finance center was established, registered with the government as the Buseesa Community Development Centre, commonly known as BCDC. Financed by seed money from benefactors in California, members of St. Julie Billiart Parish in Newbury Park and the Esseff Foundation, the Center provides small loans to people from the area in order to start "cottage industries." By 2010, approximately 100 individuals – mostly poor women, the sole support of their families – had taken advantage of this service.

As elsewhere, the sisters' presence soon drew young women to religious life. On September 8, 2002 three candidates, Amony Mary, Namugga Immaculate and Musimenta Ruth were welcomed into the newly opened Formation House in Buseesa. Four years later, on October 7, 2006, after completing their postulancy and novitiate in Tanzania, Sister Mary Immaculate and Sister Mary Amony professed their vows as the first Ugandan Sisters of Notre Dame.

At first, Ugandan young women received their initial introduction to life as a Sister of Notre Dame in Buseesa under the guidance of Sister Antoinette Marie Moon. In 2010, however, the formation program moved to Mpala, to the newly opened House of Studies. Mpala's proximity to the capital city of Kampala meant that the candidates as well as the temporary professed sisters would be able to continue their education at the local colleges and universities. At the same time a second house on the property became a hospitality house for men and women religious on their way to and from the airport in Kampala. Plans are currently underway for a learning center on the grounds in order to provide preschool instruction and child care for the young children of the town.

Rosa Mystica Today

We stand at the threshold of a new chapter in our personal, province, and congregational histories, looking to the past with gratitude, to the present with generosity, and to the future with hope. Enriched by our individual gifts, we hope to witness God's loving providence to one another, to our collaborators, and to those we serve.

Engaged with the critical social issues of our time, the Sisters of Notre Dame are actively building up of the reign of God through their diverse ministries.

Sponsored Institutions:
- Notre Dame Academy Elementary
- Notre Dame Academy
- La Reina High School
- St. Julie School, Buseesa Uganda
- Notre Dame Academy, Buseesa
- Notre Dame Learning Center, Thousand Oaks

Other Educational Ministries:
- St. Helen, South Gate
- St. Dominic, Eagle Rock
- St. Matthias High School
- St. Jude, Westlake
- St. Hedwig, Los Alamitos
- St. Rose of Lima, Simi Valley

Pastoral Ministries
- Our Lady of Grace, Encino
- Sacred Heart, Ventura
- St. Dominic, Eagle Rock
- St. Philip the Apostle, Pasadena
- St. Cornelius, Long Beach
- St. Paschal Baylon, Thousand Oaks
- St. Mel Parish, Woodland Hills

Social Ministries:
- LAMP – Board of Directors
- CAST Women's Shelter

Archdiocesan Ministries:
- St. John's Seminary
- Juan Diego House College Seminary
- Marriage Tribunal
- Cathedral Archivist/Historical Records

Health Care
- University of Southern California
  Medical Center – Transplant Program
- Hollywood Presbyterian Medical Center
- Chaplain, Queens Care
- Chaplain, California Hospital, Los Angeles

Spirituality
- Notre Dame Creations
- Associate Program
- Eucharistic Adoration

Community Support Services:
- Receptionists/office administrative staff
- Province/congregational leadership positions
- Sacristans
- Vocation/Formation Personnel

Volunteer Outreach:
- Many Mansions
- Project Achieve
- Catechist Formation/Faith Formation
- Spiritual Direction
- Life Teen
- Detention Ministry/Get on the Bus

The members of Rosa Mystica Province look forward to shaping our future as women of hope nourished by Word and Eucharist, vowed to live prophetically, committed to minister faithfully, transforming the world.

And so the Fire continues to spread.

Sr. Louise Marie Hlavac, Sr. Mary Bernadette Pendola,
Sr. Antoinette Marie Moon, Sr Marie Jeronimo Choi,
Sr. Mary Grace Leung, Sr. Shawn Marie Doyle,
Sr. Mary Kathleen Burns

Sr. Valerie Marie Roxburgh, Sister Mary Emilie Ann Palladino,
Sr. Margaret Mary Scott, Sr. Julie Marie Arriaga,
Sr. Jan Marie Villalobos

Sr. Mary Therese Kirstein, Sr. Mary Karlynn Werth,
Sr. Gina Marie Blunck, Sr. Mary Lisa Megaffin

Sr. Mary LaReina Kelly, Sr. Mary Ann Hanson, Sr. Mary Rose
Anthony Ballard (seated), Sr. Mary Josanne Furey,
Sr. Mary Donnamay Weigler (seated), Sr. Mary Joyanne Sullivan,
Sr. Mary John Shin, Sr. Mary Anita Hornack (seated),
Sr. Mary Antonine, Manning

Sr. Mary Paulynne Tubick, Sr. Cristina Marie Buczkowski,
Sr. Dwina Marie Towle (seated), Sr. Mary Regina Robbins,
Sr. Mary Angela Lee, Sr. Mary Colette Theobald,
Sr. Mary Francelia Klingshirn (seated), Sr. Carol Marie Papet,
Sr. Mary Rosaria Park

Sr. Mary Frances Wahl, Sr. Mary Teresita Keliher, Sr. Marie Paul
Grech, Sr. Donna Marie Appert

*Sr. Anna Maria Vasquez, Sr. Mary Anncarla Costello,
Sr. Mary Judeen Julier, Sr. Mary Domnic Jones*

*Sr. Rose Marie Tulacz, Sr. Mary Joann Schlarbaum, Sr. Betty Mae
Bienlein, Sr. Mary Lynn Liederbach (seated), Sr. Mary Joanne
Wittenburg, Sr. Mary Luellen Boeglin (seated), Sr. Mary Leanne
Hubbard, Sr. Florette Marie Adams*

Sr. Mary Jolisa Lazaro, Sr. Mary Richardlyn Jones, Sr. Shirley Marie McGovern, Sr. Mary Sheila Fay (seated), Sr. Mary Joan Schlotfeldt, Sr. Jane Marie McHugh, Sr. Mary Rebekah Kennedy

Sr. Mary Amy Hauck

Sr. Mary Clara Rolling

Sr. Mary Immaculette Moose

Sr. Mary Kristin Battles